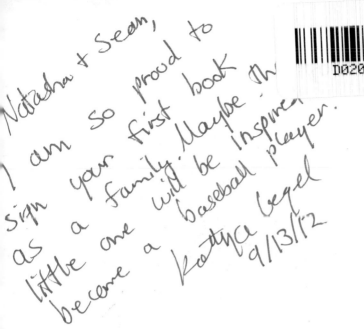

Natasha + Sean,
I am so proud to
sign your first book
as a family. Maybe the
little one will be inspired.
become a baseball player!

Katya Cengel
9/13/12

A Year in the
Minor League Life

Katya Cengel

University of Nebraska Press
Lincoln and London

Library of Congress Cataloging-in-Publication Data

Cengel, Katya.
Bluegrass baseball: a year in the minor league life / Katya Cengel.
p. cm.
Includes bibliographical references.
ISBN 978-0-8032-3535-9 (pbk.: alk. paper)
1. Minor league baseball—Kentucky—Louisville. I. Title.
GV863.K42L64   2012
796.357'640976944—dc23
2012007298

Set in Adobe Caslon by Bob Reitz.
Designed by Mikah Tacha.

Bluegrass Baseball

Bluegrass
Baseball

To Marcus, for always being there when I need him

Contents

Illustrations

Acknowledgments

When David Daley, my editor at the *Louisville Courier-Journal*, first approached me about following several Minor League Baseball players over a season, I was a little skeptical. I am a features writer, and I don't normally cover professional athletes. But then I got to know the players and the world of Minor League Baseball and realized it was the perfect setting for the kind of stories I love telling, those about regular people.

Robert Taylor believed, as I did, that the subject could be expanded into a great book and walked me through it. The teams made it all possible, with Tom Gauthier, Nick Evans, Keith Elkins, Megan Smith, and Josh Anderson helping to coordinate my trips.

Of course, without the players, presidents, and managers, there would have been nothing to write. I am grateful to them for letting me into their lives. Then there are the family members, fans, ushers, host families, and other people who were so generous with their time and stories.

Photographers James Calvert and Alex Slitz captured the images I hope I conveyed in words. My mother and stepfather provided valuable feedback and support, and my sister, friends, and other family members helped me in every way they could.

But the most important was Marcus, who has all the patience I lack and helped me in more ways than I can list.

Introduction

In many ways, the story of independent and Minor League Baseball in Kentucky is the story of baseball. It is a tale of dreams, history, and heartache.

There are the former Major Leaguers who spent their early professional careers in little mountain towns—Greg Maddux, Dan Plesac, and Dwight Smith. Before they were in the bigs, all three played for Minor League teams in eastern Kentucky, where attendance sometimes didn't even reach the triple digits.[1] Bobby Flynn helped establish the first integrated team in the South when he, a white man, joined the black semiprofessional Lexington Hustlers in 1947.[2] Let's not forget Louisville, the state's largest city, where professional baseball has been a part of things for well over a century and whose Minor League Louisville Colonels nurtured such talents as Hall of Famers Earle Combs, Joe McCarthy, and Harold "Pee Wee" Reese, who embraced Jackie

Robinson when he broke Major League Baseball's color line.[3]

But that is just the background in which this book is set. The action takes place during the 2010 season, as three Minor and one independent league teams battle for fans, wins, and a future here in the Bluegrass.

These men are professionals—they are paid to play—but life for them is nothing like it is for their colleagues in the bigs. They are paid a fraction of what their Major League counterparts make, travel mostly by bus, and live with constant uncertainty, all in the belief that it will pay off down the road. But even among the best of them, the ones drafted, only about 5 percent to 10 percent will make it to the Majors.[4]

Some will never get past the first level, Rookie League. If they do, there is still Class-A Short-Season, Class-A (including high and low or advanced and regular), AA, and AAA. With more than a dozen leagues and almost two hundred teams that charge admission, the Minor League system is an immense maze through which some players never make it.[5] But at least they are on the fast track, playing for a team affiliated with a Major League club. Players in the independent league have no such affiliation; they are a step below even the Minors. Down here the game is different; general managers in the Minor and independent leagues talk more about affordable family entertainment than winning. It's a business, and they are in the business of developing players and running a successful local operation.

The stories that hover around these lower-level teams are populated by characters trying to reach a goal, or keep one from slipping away. These are kids right out of high school living away from home for the first time, athletes from poor countries trying to find something better, and men well into their twenties struggling to hold on to the one thing they know.

And that's just the players. In the Minors you have managers who missed making the Majors now living a life just as exhausting as their players. They do it without the hope of fame, however, just to keep the taste of the sport in their system. There are wives who live their lives in limbo so their husbands can chase their dreams and children whose home is the road and whose toys must fit in a small storage container. There are also the fans, businesspeople, and politicians who brought the teams to town, the families that welcome players into their homes, and the entertainers who keep the crowds coming.

The characters who populate Kentucky's three Minor and one independent league teams include all of these and more. The Class-A Lexington Legends have a colorful president whose wife is an equally colorful state senator. Alan Stein is baseball in Lexington. If it wasn't for Alan, this Houston Astros farm team would not exist. Lexington has a spotty history with professional baseball, and several attempts to bring a team to the city before Alan met with failure. Instead of waiting for the city to fund the ballpark, Alan found investors and set to work. He has eaten cat food, slept in the stands, shaved his head, and endured a number of other hardships to keep his name in the spotlights and fans in the stands.

But as the team embarks on its tenth season, general manager Andy Shea, a former college baseball player, is playing more of an active role in the team's story. Hanging around the periphery of this story is Freddy Acevedo, a former player who followed his dream from the Dominican Republic only to watch it slip away in Lexington, far from the Majors and his home.

Toby Rumfield is closer to his dream. The Major League team that picked him in the second round of the 1991 draft is just across the Ohio River in Cincinnati. But Rumfield isn't playing anymore; he is managing a team in Florence that is at the bottom of the bottom, a team that isn't even tied to a Major League team. This is where players go when they have been overlooked or released. This is their first stop on the way up or their last stop on the way down.

Rumfield's wife, Kari, is general manager here. Their three children are along for the ride, falling asleep in the stands, serving as bat boys and snack vendors. Baseball here is as close and as far as many fans will ever get to the stars of tomorrow. Spring training is here, not in Florida, and players live with local families, not in extended-stay hotels.

But it isn't quite as cozy as you might think. The team's original owner spent time in prison, and the team was in danger of falling into nonexistence until local businessman Clint Brown came to the rescue.

Restaurateur Rick Kelley and Warren County judge executive Mike Buchanon, the top elected leader of the county, didn't have to rescue the Bowling Green Hot Rods. They created them. The Class-A Tampa Bay Rays team was a key part of the city's downtown revitalization now under way. The team played its first season in 2009, right in the middle of one of the worst recessions in decades. The ballpark was built in about a year, the staff hired on the fly, the players brought in before there was a clubhouse. Now they are opening their second season and doing their best to build a fan base in a city that has little history of professional baseball.

Louisville's baseball history stretches back more than a century and remains present in places like the Louisville Slugger Museum & Factory and Pee Wee Reese Road. This is where players go before the Majors, AAA, the last stop on the long road to the top, in this case the Cincinnati Reds. By the time they arrive here, they may have wives and children. One day off a month, pay far below that of their Major League counterparts, and little security have begun to take their toll. The true stars sometimes skip AAA and go from AA to the Majors. Louisville is where players decide if it is worth it. It is also where Mary E. Barney spent twenty-five years working her way from receptionist to director of baseball operations.

These are the teams, and this is their story. There are few record breakers here or amazing statistics, just ordinary people who may someday become extraordinary, but may just as likely disappear into the annals of history.

In these cities, for these players and the people who watch and support them, baseball isn't a sport but a way of life, a childhood dream that just might come true. Over a season that dream can be derailed by injuries, debts, or bad timing. It can be made and then lost in the next game. This isn't the world of chartered planes and huge fame; this is the world of leaking roofs and sales calls made on cell phones while sitting on buckets. This is where it all begins, and, for many, where it ends.

Bluegrass Baseball

Part 1
Lexington Legends:
A Tale of Obsession

1. The Legend behind the Legends

I needed one man. But he wasn't sure he needed me. Convincing Kentucky's other Minor League Baseball teams to let me follow them for the season was easy. The team's public relations representative told the manager they needed to cooperate. And they did. That wasn't how it worked with the Lexington Legends. Only Alan Stein could grant me access to the team, and so far it didn't look like I would make it past his office.

Alan sat behind his desk, a classic southern old-boy type, or so I thought, with a mustache, several large shiny rings, suspenders, and a big belly. His schedule is kept by a secretary, and his oldest son is named Wade, after the Confederate Civil War soldier Wade Hampton. But his youngest son is named Scooter, after the late Hall of Fame Yankees shortstop Phil Rizzuto, nicknamed the Scooter. As I quickly figured out, although Alan wasn't impressed by the idea of being in a book—he had already been in one—he was impressed that I knew something about Minor League Baseball. Later I would discover just how far he was willing to go for the sport, but right then all I needed to know was that I was in with Alan, the Legends' president.

Alan wasn't always the man in charge. Growing up Jewish in the South in the mid-twentieth century meant the only way he could play golf at the local country club was by sneaking in through a hole in the fence. No blacks. No Jews. When Alan's dad was invited to be the first Jewish member, he turned them down. He didn't want to be a token. His eldest child has no such qualms about being referred to as the face of the Legends. Alan is now chief operating officer of a management company that owns multiple Minor League Baseball teams in addition to the Legends, but in a way the Legends are still his, and he is still the Legends. He is obsessed. He had to be to do what he did.

But I wouldn't realize that until later. It was still February, and the first big competition was not between athletes on a field but between singers at the Fayette Mall in Lexington. There are no bats, no balls, and not much testosterone. Instead there is a temporary stage, hovering mothers, dolled-up teens, and the Beaumont Quartet. This is the quartet's third year at the Legends' annual national anthem tryouts, and they are pretty much guaranteed success. Not only did they make the cut the past two years, but they also have a winning record—both times they performed, the Class-A Legends won the game. So they are far from fazed by the competition gathered at the mall this Sunday afternoon.

They are also of an age where they see the tryouts for what they are—a chance to sing at a Minor League Baseball game—and not a jump-start on the road to fame. They already have careers, or, in the case of Bob Hooker, had them. Bob is fifty-nine and retired. Mark and Frieda Gebert are professors in their midforties and fifties, and Frieda's sister, Kathy Shewmaker, is a "fiftyish" grade school teacher.

The singing started about a decade ago when they took part in a Christmas show at the nearby Beaumont Inn. They read about the Legends' auditions three years ago and figured "it could be a hoot," says Frieda.

"We like baseball," adds her sister, Kathy.

Mark may like it a little too much. In addition to the anthem tryouts, Mark has tried out to be a public address announcer for the Legends for the past two years. He didn't make it. But then for years Alan had no success in bringing a professional baseball team to town. He didn't give up. And neither will Mark. Mark does not say he failed as an announcer, just that he did not make it.

"Not yet," says Frieda.

"Not yet," echoes Kathy.

"Not yet, but he could show you the scar," continues Frieda.

She isn't kidding about the scar—or about making Mark reveal it. It turns out that while driving to the PA announcer auditions last year, Mark was in a car accident. He ended up with a steel plate in his left shoulder. After he was released from the emergency room, he went to Applebee's Park to audition. The tryouts had long since ended, but the Legends staff agreed to hear him out. Their sympathy extended only so far, though, because Mark didn't make the cut.

The cut in his left shoulder left a "nice" scar, Frieda says, pulling back her husband's blue polo shirt. "It was a heck of a wreck." Mark isn't sure if the Legends are holding PA announcer auditions this year. "And if they do, I may not let him [go]," says Frieda.

"Or drive him anyway," adds Kathy.

They share a laugh, and then Frieda gets serious, pulling the group together and leading them toward the stage, four middle-aged men and women in black dress pants and blue polo shirts. They are the first to perform, and they are good—so good you almost forget the whole thing is taking place in the walkway between Payless Shoe Source and Caramel Carnival snack store.

The afternoon stretches on, and countless others belt out the anthem. There is a young man whose voice breaks part-way through. He doesn't bother finishing, just steps down and disappears into the Sunday mall traffic. There is a teenage girl whose high is so high little kids passing by on the way to Dick's Sporting Goods cover their ears and scrunch their faces. Then there are those who sing so beautifully that even though you have heard dozens of anthems in the past few hours, you stop and listen. Those are the ones Alan, one of several people judging the event, awards straight tens. Then he leans back in his chair and listens. They are the ones who cause a young couple to stop midstride, grasp hands, and watch.

Dorsey Franklin isn't quite one of them. But she is something. Dressed in a sailor costume, with blonde hair and a voice far bigger than you expect from a nine-year-old, she is an audience favorite. And she seems to know it. Her rendition is not perfect, but it is hard to ignore, with her tight white pants, tasseled top, Orphan Annie pipes, and matching hand gestures.

Offstage her mother, Lucille, holds Dorsey's monogrammed pink bags. Dorsey has been singing since she was six and has been practicing the anthem with her voice coach for the past three weeks. "We really should have taken longer, I think, but we didn't know about it in time," says Lucille. They heard about the tryouts from a friend. And for three weeks' practice, both mother and daughter are pleased with the results, pleased enough they may stop by Dorsey's favorite restaurant, Golden Corral, on the way home.

At the judge's table Alan also seems happy. And not just with Dorsey's performance. This is the second and last day of tryouts, and all of the two hundred audition spots have been filled. When Alan showed up a half hour before the day's events were set to begin, an employee complained that she couldn't accommodate all the people showing up without appointments. Alan smiled, unfazed. They have seventy home games, with a different national anthem singer at each game, but the tryouts are about more than just finding singers. They are about being able to "touch the community," generating excitement for the club, and, of course, providing entertainment.

It's the reason behind pretty much everything he does, because Alan Stein is the Legends, from the burly mascot with the handlebar mustache, not unlike Alan's own mustache, to the design of the stadium and the preseason gimmicks. It all comes out of Alan's head. And now, ten years after it all began, he is still the guy behind professional baseball in Lexington. "The guy everybody said couldn't have baseball in town, couldn't do it without public money" is how the announcer introduces Alan at the auditions.

Whether you like him or not, and most like him, pretty much everyone agrees Alan is the reason the Legends are in Lexington. And he isn't shy about telling you the story of how he got them here. It is a story as entertaining as the sport he promotes, because if Alan understands one thing, it is that Minor League Baseball is about entertainment.

But before the story of the Legends is the story of Alan. He takes his time telling it, speaking slowly so you don't miss a word. He starts with his paternal grandparents, who hail from Lithuania. From there he moves to his father, a World War II veteran with an entrepreneurial spirit that led him to the restaurant, barbecue wholesale, and construction businesses, among others.

The oldest of five, Alan grew up working in the family restaurant. But he didn't just work with what his father had started. He had his own projects as well. The first was a bar near the University of Kentucky, located in downtown Lexington. As a student at UK, Alan had noticed that there were plenty of places to get a beer around campus, but few where you could find a cocktail. So he opened one and called it 803 South. After that there was real estate, radio, and, finally, baseball.

"Alan's very visionary," said his sister, Teri Stein Harper. "He can see things others cannot."

In the 1980s when Alan read about talk of a Major League Baseball expansion, which would probably mean an expansion for Minor League Baseball as well, he saw it as an opportunity to bring the sport to his hometown. So he started an advocacy group devoted to just that.

There had been professional baseball in Lexington before. The city had a team in the Blue Grass League from the league's inception in 1908 to its demise following the 1912 season.[1] The league started as an independent league but joined the National Association of Professional Baseball Leagues in 1909 and was designated a Minor League Class-D League—out of A, B, C, or D, based on the city's population. In 1913 the team joined the Ohio State League, also Class-D, and stayed with it until that league disbanded in 1916. Tough times followed for the world, and Minor League Baseball and professional baseball did not return to Lexington until 1922, when the Blue Grass League was revived and Lexington joined once again, playing in it until 1924. Lexington had a team in the Kentucky-Illinois-Tennessee (better known as KITTY) League Class-D level from 1935 to 1938 and in 1954 played one season in the Mountain States League, which at the time was a Class-C level.[2]

But for much of recent history there was no professional baseball in Lexington. Bringing it back was the sort of thing many dreamed of, the kind of thing older successful businessmen talk about when they have time and cash to spare. The only difference is that Alan stuck it out for more than a decade to make sure it came true. There were those who said it couldn't be done, those who figured he would give up. Then there were those who knew Alan.

"He was the one guy willing to just kind of drive through all that junk, all the naysayers saying you can't do it," explained Chuck Mraz, news director of nearby Morehead State Public Radio. "He said, 'To heck with that, we're gonna do it.'"

And he did. Sitting in an old storage area that has been converted into his office at Applebee's Park, Alan is in his element. The baseball caps he has collected over the years decorate his high office walls, photos of famous players posing with his family rest on his desk, and a Cracker Jack box sits in a planter. When his phone rings he takes the calls reluctantly, drumming his fingers on his desk impatiently, holding the phone away from his head dramatically and repeating, "Right, yeah, right, yeah, right, yep, yep . . ."

The baseball field has become Alan's stage. While he says he leaves a lot to his general manager, Andy Shea, he has yet to exit the theater. It isn't the role he imagined himself playing as a child. Back then, like so many other little boys, he wanted to be a baseball player. But in a way his role now is even better, because he is a player on a higher level. He may not ever be the guy to score the winning run, or pitch the perfect game for the

Legends, but he knows without him, there probably wouldn't be a Legends team.

It's not that Kentucky's second-largest city isn't a sports town. It is—there is University of Kentucky basketball and University of Kentucky football, in that order. Fans and most residents take both seriously, which means during March, not a lot gets done around there. Then there is horse racing. Lexington sits deep in horse country, rolling hills with white and black fences behind which run thoroughbreds and blue bloods.

Before becoming president of a baseball team, Alan was president of a local synagogue and estimates the Jewish population to number about a thousand or so in a city of nearly three hundred thousand. But religion was never a problem. Government was—at least that's how Alan tells it. Never mind the fact that his wife, Kathy, is a state senator.

In the years after Alan formed his advocacy group, several important steps were taken to bring professional baseball to Kentucky. In the late 1980s the mayor and city council were approached about building the stadium needed for a Minor League team. In 1991 the commissioner of Major League Baseball, Faye Vincent, paid the city a visit. In 1996 Lexington was pitched as a potential Minor League franchise location. Nothing happened. Meanwhile, in other states around the nation, cities and counties were building new stadiums. Alan and his partners continued to push the city for support, believing Lexington would be like other communities where the government took the lead in getting a stadium built. "And that just didn't happen here," says Alan.

At least three times the public was told Lexington was going to get a team, but each time public funding for a new stadium fell through. Even a state surplus that resulted in a number of statewide capital projects did not help secure the $12 million or so needed. Alan explains, without bitterness, that Kathy was a member of the state legislature that did not vote to prioritize a baseball stadium for use of the funds. As he sees it, either Lexington was a leader in refusing to fund the stadium, or "you could say they missed the boat." Either way, by the late 1990s he knew if there was going to be a baseball stadium, he was going to have to find another way to fund it.

He had no doubt that the venture would be profitable. When the spring horse racing meet at Keeneland and UK basketball end, there isn't much going on until UK football starts in the fall. Plus, there is no riverfront or lakefront in Lexington, all of which in Alan's mind added up to no real competition. He also had the time and money to work on the project, having sold his radio stations in 1998. So he decided to fund the project privately, becoming one of the first fully privately funded stadiums that relied on individuals, not a foundation.

Of course, it wasn't easy. For a while even Alan didn't think he could do it. For a AA team in the Southern Franchise, they would need to build a stadium with at least six thousand seats and pay $7.5 million in franchise costs. They didn't have the money.

But when Alan's then seven-year-old son, Scooter, challenged him to do the math, he started thinking. He couldn't afford a AA team, but a Class-A team was another story, with a stadium that required only four thousand seats and franchise costs of $3.5 million.

All of a sudden, Alan's business model worked. The problem was that everyone kept telling him people in Lexington wouldn't support a Class-A team; they would only watch a AA team that played against teams from similar-size cities. Plus, if they were AA, they had a chance of being an affiliate of the nearby Major League Cincinnati Reds.

Alan didn't think people cared. To prove it he and his team surveyed spectators at other Minor League facilities, mainly the AA Southern League franchise in Chattanooga, Tennessee. What they found was that 52 percent of people coming out of the games "didn't give a damn about who won the game; 52 percent didn't even know the score of the games," says Alan. More than 60 percent did not know what level of baseball they had just seen, with some offering some pretty crazy answers, like Japanese League, Little League, and even Major League. As for Major League affiliation, 70-some percent didn't know who the team was affiliated with. But 98 percent did know they had a good time and would come back. When asked why, their answers had less to do with baseball than with economics and convenience—in other words, it was cheap, clean, and convenient fun.

All of which gave Alan enough fuel to talk twenty-two different investors into forking over about $12 million. The first man he got on board was his good friend Billy Forbess. A Lexington dentist, Billy didn't have much faith in the project. He was not even a baseball fan. But he was an "Alan fan," and from day one he has had season tickets right beside Alan. "I know he has a hundred best friends, but he's my best friend," said Billy. Alan's ability to make everybody feel like his best friend is one of the things that makes him such a successful businessman, said Billy. And Billy insisted with Alan that it is sincere, not some sleazy salesman trick. He has known Alan more than thirty-five years and has seen him make financial sacrifices in order to protect other businessmen.

After Billy others followed. The biggest investor was Brad Redmon, a successful local entrepreneur who put in about $5 million. Alan was the second-largest investor, with about $1.5 million. They still needed about $10 million more. And no big banks wanted to take the risk.

The Bank of Lexington isn't big. It is a small local bank that did not have the kind of money Alan and his partners needed. But it could be the lead bank of a consortium of smaller banks, and that's what happened. The Bank of Lexington put together eleven little banks that together could lend the money. "So that was it. That's how we got it done," Alan says.

But he isn't done. There are a lot more tales to tell, and the calls coming into his office are dismissed quickly. A large man with a cut-to-the-chase manner, Alan can appear intimidating, until he starts talking about himself. Then he is just a well-dressed fifty-eight-year-old reminiscing about the biggest adventure of his life, an adventure that in the beginning felt a lot like the "Wild, Wild West," he says. "There were plenty of times along the way when I said to myself, 'I don't know how I'm going to make this next construction draw tomorrow. Where am I going to get $600,000 tomorrow?' you know."

Contractors threatened to stop work, but all the time the group kept selling tickets and advertising. In February 2000, fifteen months before they would play their first game, in a stadium that wasn't built, for a team they didn't own yet, to a league that they didn't belong, they started selling season tickets. They sold almost two thousand on the first day. And they weren't just selling for the first season. One of the conditions of their loan was that season-ticket holders, sponsors, and advertisers had to commit for a minimum of three years. The Legends tried to extend things even more by offering discounts for even longer commitments, which many took them up on. The founding corporate sponsors signed on for ten years. It wasn't a hard sell. "We spent so much effort and energy on creating this dream that it became a community dream," Alan says. "It wasn't just mine. Everybody was on board."

These long-term investments ensured not only that the venture would live past the excitement of the "honeymoon" first season, but that it would survive in general. You see, the League Championship Series in which the Legends were supposed to play was canceled following the September 11, 2001, attacks. While the rest of the nation was struggling in the aftermath of the terrorist attacks, the Legends actually saw their revenues go up in 2002, because everything was already locked in and anything sold beyond that was a plus, says Alan. And they sold beyond that. Alan is not content to coast on any early success; he stands in the spotlight drawing attention to his team.

The first year it was cat food. The season opener that year was against the Alley Cats in Charleston, West Virginia. Talking trash before the game, Alan guaranteed the Legends would win or he would eat cat food. The press loved it, especially when the Legends lost and they got photos of the team president eating cat food. Alan can't recall exactly how much he shoveled down, or whether it was dry or wet—he thinks he ate about a can of the dry stuff—but there is no forgetting the attention the whole episode generated. And for him that is what counts; what he has to go through is irrelevant, so long as it benefits the team.

"I mean, he's willing to go the extra mile even though it might prove to be a little bit personally disastrous. It always works out well from a PR standpoint," said Chuck Mraz of Morehead State Public Radio.

The cat food stunt was the best advertising the Legends never paid for, so the following year Alan decided to do something again, this time before the Legends' first home game. Back then his hair was long and bushy, so he decided he would guarantee a win or he would shave his head. Of course, they lost, and Alan lost his hair. Well, kind of. "I still have the hair right here," he says, pulling a plastic bag filled with brown hair from his desk. He keeps the hair as a reminder of all the fun he had as a bald man. His shaved head generated so much interest that he started charging advertisers to have their logos painted on it. The first night he charged one hundred dollars; by the fourth, and last, night, he was up to eight hundred. Ten years later people still stop him on the street and comment on how his hair has grown back.

The third year's stunt went even further, and almost cost him his marriage. He had just undergone major surgery for colon cancer a few weeks before opening night and guaranteed the team would win or he would sit in his seat, section 207, row 6, seat 12, until they did. He was allowed to leave to go to the bathroom, but that was it. "I thought my wife was going to divorce me, to tell you the truth, and my doctor was going to shoot me," he says.

They lost the first night, which was okay, because it was about seventy-four degrees and a large fan base supplied Alan with food and soft drinks. The next night, they lost again and a cold front came through, bringing with it gusting winds and hail. A local outdoor outfitter brought Alan a tent and sleeping bag. In the morning, radio and television station weather helicopters circled the park to show that Alan was still there, and the *Lexington Herald-Leader* newspaper got a picture of Alan waking up. "He waited an hour until I woke up so he could take a photograph as soon as I opened my eyes. It made front page," laughs Alan.

He calculates that the stunt probably brought in about five hundred thousand dollars in free media. The third night the weather was miserable again, and the Legends were behind by three runs in the bottom of the ninth with two outs and nobody on. Then they got a hit, followed by another hit, and things started to turn around, with the Legends pulling through for a win. It was their only win that home stand.

Alan ended up back in the hospital. But that, he smiles, is another story, and does not matter. His wife, Kathy, sees it a little differently. "I tried to get him to come in," she said. "He wouldn't." He was recovering from cancer treatment, she added, and for anyone else that would be explanation enough. Not for Alan. She knows that now, knows not to even try to change him. But she is still his wife, and she still worries. "To see him work so hard," she said. "He really just puts his nose to the grindstone, starting fifteen years ago, and he continues to do it."

He has fun, of course. At least he makes sure it looks like he is having fun, but being an entertainer is hard work. The year after the bleachers stint, he came up with a new plan. After three years of losing his bets, he decided to blame the losses on the bat boy and promised fans that if the team lost the home opener, he would take over the bat boy's duties until they won. Of course, they lost, which, Alan is quick to add, was great in those days. Fans love a win, but they also love seeing the team president make a fool of himself. As a bat boy he donned the uniform, but instead of resting on a bucket, he lounged on a Barcalounger reclining chair.

He did that for two nights. Eventually, the Legends started winning their home openers, saving Alan and his general manger from wearing Batman and Robin costumes, among other humiliations. Then they won a few more, and Alan let front-office general manager Andy Shea choose the gimmicks. Those weren't quite as outlandish, according to Alan, so this year Alan is back in full form, offering to shave his distinctive white mustache if the Legends lose their home opener. Kathy didn't have much to say on that one. She has learned not to interfere. "He is his own man," she said. But she crossed her fingers it wouldn't happen. She has never seen him without a mustache and didn't really want to experience that.

The national anthem auditions are another crowd pleaser the Legends put on every year. The first few years they took place over three days, lasted twenty hours, and drew as many as six hundred people. Now the Legends office staff spends two days and a total of six hours listening to about two hundred performers. Out of those they will choose fewer than seventy, leaving some spots open for celebrities and other surprise appearances.

The judging is left to a panel consisting of the team's media sponsors and a representative from the team, which this year is Alan. The whole thing is so Alan, it would almost feel as if something was missing if he wasn't there. Each judge is given a sheet on which they rate performances based on lyrical accuracy, vocal quality, presentation, voice projection, and overall performance. Then there are what Alan calls the intangibles; little kids, instrumentals, and big groups of kids always score high with audiences and thus also with Alan.

Whether they make it or not, every contestant will receive a thank you letter. Those who make it will be given a list of dates to choose from on which to perform. Those who don't will be given a voucher for two tickets to a Legends game.

Jonathan Hagee got the tickets last year. He came in regular clothes. This year, the fifty-two-year-old software project manager looks like a pilgrim dressed in colonial reenactor garb, complete with knee socks and buckle shoes. When he got a call from the Legends asking him to return this year, he decided to go all out and don his reenactor garb. It seems to have worked, for after his performance Alan pulls Jonathan aside and tells him if he gets picked to wear what he is wearing. Still, the anthem is difficult and a departure from what he usually does—traditional Irish and Scottish ballads. "But everyone knows this song, right?" Jonathan says. "It's just converting what's in your head to your voice."

Or in Miles Osland's case, it is converting it to your saxophone. The director of jazz studies and a professor of saxophone at UK, Miles has performed annually at a Legends game since they have been around. He also does UK football and basketball games. He doesn't do it for the money, he jokes, because there isn't any. He does it because if your name is Miles, then you'd better play sax. Playing it at a Minor League Baseball game is bound to draw exposure to the musical program where you work. One of Miles's students taught Alan's son Scooter in high school. Scooter was doing well, he says. "I was sorry to see him give it up."

Miles believes that the anthem contestants have improved over the years. Luckily, not all care enough to keep their appointments, which means one little girl and her father will go home happy. The pair arrived early, but not nearly early enough. They hadn't registered in advance, and there were no openings left. But they signed onto the waiting list and sat side by side for several hours, waiting to see if they would be called.

The little girl is about eight and dressed in winter boots and leggings. When she gets word she will get to perform, she smiles and takes the stage without her father. She clasps the microphone tightly in both hands and starts off in a sweet voice that doesn't quite carry. When she stumbles over a word, a hand flies to her mouth. But she doesn't let that stop her, just gives a little smile and continues. She is a wisp of a thing with a pretty voice and a sweet, unpolished image. When she finishes, the crowd erupts in cheers. She smiles, glides off the stage, and runs into the waiting arms of her father.

2. The Man Who Would Be Alan

When people in town learn Andy's father owns the Legends, they smile in recognition. "They're like, 'Oh, Andy Stein,'" says Andy. Only his last name is Shea. His father is William Shea, owner of the Legends. But it is Alan's name and legacy Andy bumps up against in Lexington. He may be the front-office general manager, but at the national anthem tryouts, his presence was barely noted. When his opening-day stunts didn't meet Alan's approval, they were taken away. They won't return this season or the next.

Standing in Alan's office, Andy looks young and obedient as Alan questions him about an upcoming appearance. But in his own office, Andy runs the show, ignoring knocks at the door when he doesn't feel like answering them and setting strict rules on punctuality and eating. "I have banned food from meetings, and I cannot stand it when people are late," he says. "Sometimes I'll lock the damn door right at the time."

And while Alan leaves little time for himself, Andy takes time to hang out with friends and work out. Right now he is getting over an injured pectoral muscle. He was bench pressing, and as he was bringing the barbell down to his chest, his muscle "popped." It was a torn labrum and rotator cuff almost a decade earlier that ended his baseball-playing career. He was a catcher and outfielder at Boston College when he messed up his shoulder. He finished the season, but never returned to baseball—as a player, at least. "I was like, if I'm not going to be playing, I definitely sure as hell want to work in baseball," he says from his office near first base at Applebee's Park.

And that is how he ended up here, on a Thursday afternoon in early June, six years after he graduated from Boston College with a marketing and human resources degree. He has been general manager three years and with the team six. He is twenty-eight, single, and hell bent on showing the people of this rather conservative southern town how to have a good time.

Raised for the most part in Philadelphia and of Irish extraction, Andy chose Boston College not just because of baseball, but also because of its social scene. When he came to Lexington after graduation, he was dismayed to discover how lacking his social options were. There was the college scene and the forty-plus scene, but nothing much in-between. That left him with the option of hanging out in a college bar or going to a "low-key place" that closed at midnight, neither of which he found appealing.

But all of that has changed, and he isn't shy about mentioning the role he believes he has played in that change. One of the things he is most proud of as front-office general manager of the Legends is the number and size of non-Legends events he has brought to the ballpark, events like mixed martial arts fights, beer festivals, and mainstream country music concerts. Because all these events take place when the Legends are on the road, they provide more entertainment for young people and a chance for the Legends' parent company, which owns the stadium, to make extra money while also drawing attention to the team. If people coming from elsewhere in the state for a concert at the park note how nice the venue is, they may be tempted to check out what the venue's main tenant is all about, says Andy, which is "huge to us."

Then there are the downtown clubs and bars that keep popping up, including his own. It hasn't opened yet—doesn't even have a name—but today Andy signed the lease on a vacant building on West Main Street he and his business partner plan to turn into a bar. The idea, he says, is for it not only to appeal to "the Alans of the world, who still go out, have a good time, but are not looking to go clubbing and whatever else, but also, as the night goes on, to be able to appeal to the me's of the world." He doesn't mention his father; he mentions Alan. He can't escape him; even his club idea is haunted by Alan. The landlord was one of those people who became confused on learning Andy's father owned the Legends. He thought Alan did. Then there is the fact that when he was younger, Alan had his own bar.

Andy didn't hit on inspiration the same way Alan did, and he plans to leave the day-to-day running of the place to his partner. He comes in more on the investment side. Owning a bar wasn't something he had always dreamed of doing, but when his business partner showed him the downtown spot four months ago, he thought it was too good a location and opportunity to pass up. They hoped to open by fall, in time for the 2010 Alltech FEI World Equestrian Games being held in Lexington.

But aside from the bar, party-boy image, and focus on social events at Applebee's Park, Shea can be thoughtful. He is a huge fan of the late Pat Tillman, the professional football player who enlisted in the army after September 11 and died in Afghanistan in 2004. On the wall of his office, Andy keeps a framed *Sports Illustrated* cover of Tillman posed in a tree with a gun. At home he keeps another of Tillman in a football jersey. Despite his talent, Tillman was humble and simple, says Andy, unlike some of the guys Andy comes across playing Class-A baseball who think they run the world. Tillman, he says, "drove a Jeep Wrangler that didn't have air-conditioning that worked. He did it because he loved the game. . . . [T]here really just aren't many people like that," says Andy. "Hell, I'm not."

He tries to be. This morning he texted his friend, a former marine questioning the morals of his new job in college sports: "You gotta do what you gotta do. Principles above everything." His friend texted back: "Yep, Tillman."

A little more than a year ago, after his twenty-seventh birthday and a weekend of partying, Andy signed up to be a big brother with the Big Brothers Big Sisters mentoring organization. "I had just spent the whole weekend partying my butt off with all my friends. My brother was in town. I was like, I need to take a step in the other direction," he says. He meets his little brother, Christian, a skinny twelve-year-old obsessed with fitness, once a week. They go to Buffalo Wild Wings and watch ESPN's *SportsCenter* together, work out in the gym at Andy's home or at the ballpark, go bowling, and hang out at baseball games. "I'd take him anywhere in the world," says Andy. "But he always wants KFC or Chick-fil-A or Buffalo Wild Wings."

They talk about sports and lifting weights, but not about homework. Andy steers clear of the weighted issues, wanting to remain more of a fun older brother than a demanding father. He has taken Christian to Legends games, and Christian got to go in the clubhouse and meet the players and meet famous athletes throwing ceremonial first pitches. Christian gets everything he wants for free at the ballpark, but he told Andy he would rather spend time with Andy somewhere else when Andy isn't working. So Andy plans to meet with him outside the ballpark, where he doesn't have to always answer his cell phone.

At the ballpark, he can't ignore his phone. After all, he is Andy Shea, and his name carries a lot of weight. It was his last name that led him to Boston College, in part. He isn't related to the John Shea that the college's Shea Field is named after, but it seemed like a sign that he would be playing baseball on a field that bore his last name.

He also isn't related to the William Shea who is credited with bringing National League Baseball back to New York City last century. But he can't escape the legacy of the William Shea who owns the Legends. Being the owner's son, he says, hurt him socially when he first joined the team. And the social element has always been important to Andy. "No one wanted to hang out with the owner's son," he says.

In 2005 his father's group, then called Fun Entertainment LLC, purchased the Legends and Applebee's Park from the original ownership group Alan had put together and of which Brad Redmon was the majority owner. Alan invested in both the selling and the purchasing groups.[1]

Andy came on board not long after his father took over. No one knew what either he or his father was like, and Andy himself wasn't sure how he was supposed to behave. His sole previous work experience was as a lifeguard.

He spent his first two and a half years as the season-ticket representative, making cold calls and even knocking on doors trying to get businesses to sign up for season tickets. He also ran the parking lot during games. "It definitely sucked," he says. But he's glad he did it because it makes it easier when employees complain about having to make forty calls or how tough it is to work parking. "It's nice being able to say it is important, it is doable, it's manageable, and I've done it," says Andy. "It's not just a bunch of schmooze."

He even has a retort when people complain about being the mascot. He got roped into that early on. Being rather small of stature, he was made to dress as Pee Wee, the baseball mascot. It is a photo of his Pee Wee that still decorates the doors of the park's bathrooms. His mom always gets a kick out of that when she and his father come for opening day and other important games.

For Andy, being a general manager during the season is a totally different job from the rest of the year. When baseball isn't being played, he is dressed in a suit and tie and working from eight in the morning to five at night. During the season he wears shorts and Nike shoes, and his hours stretch late into the night.

For Alan there isn't much of a difference. He is usually dressed smartly, and his hours are long year-round. When he vacations in South Carolina he tries to time it so he can see the Legends play in Charleston. "No such thing as vacations anymore. With the way communications are, you're always in touch," said Alan.

His friend Billy Forbess said Alan works himself into a state of exhaustion all the time. But only those closest to Alan notice when he is tired or depressed, said Billy, because Alan always appears enthusiastic, upbeat, and optimistic. And he is always thinking about baseball. "I don't think you can be a successful businessman unless you focus on it virtually 100 percent of the time," said Billy. "So of course he's had to make sacrifices in his life to be successful in his baseball career."

Andy works differently. Today he has on his plaid shorts for Thirsty Thursday, dollar-beer night. "I don't obsess over [work]," he says. "What I tell everyone, you've got to have a personal life." Even during the season Andy's thoughts stray from baseball. He pulls out a poster of country music star Jason Aldean from behind his desk. "This, I'm pretty proud of," he says. As people line up outside waiting for the gates to open, announcements for the upcoming Tim McGraw and Maroon 5 concerts are blasted over the loudspeakers.

At a shaded picnic table inside the park, shortstop Jiovanni Mier and second baseman Jose Altuve talk about life as a Legend. They are both at the same level now, but by the end of the season, one will have advanced while the other will be left behind.

Jiovanni has had a slow start this season, but he is the obvious choice to progress, the bonus baby whom the franchise will be watching closely to make sure they maximize their investment. Jio, as family and friends call him, started playing baseball at four years old and from the beginning showed such talent that he was playing with nine-year-olds when he was six and twelve-year-olds when he was nine, said his mother, Leticia Mier. Even then, when Jiovanni was playing the field, the coach had to catch for him. That rule was implemented after a kid catching for Jio got hit in the face when he was unable to hold onto the ball. "It wasn't fair for the kids to get hit, and it wasn't fair for Jiovanni to not throw the ball like he was supposed to," explained Leticia.

Jose was cheap, and less is expected of him. But Alan likes him. It wasn't the second baseman's impressive stature that caught Alan's attention. "He lists himself at five foot five. Not a chance," said Alan.

Jose is tiny, probably more like five foot three. Some say he is too small to be a great ballplayer. But he is scrappy. He hustles.

He works hard. He is all over the place. In a word, like Alan, Jose is obsessed.

Jiovanni has a girlfriend, has a family, has a fancy car; he has options. Jose has baseball. And Alan likes that about him. "He's one of my favorites this year," said Alan.

Neither Jose or Jiovanni went to college. Jiovanni is only nineteen, Jose twenty. When Jiovanni got assigned to the Houston Astros' Rookie affiliate in Greenville, Tennessee, last June, he didn't even know how to do laundry. And when he left, he still didn't. "I was only there two months, so I basically took two months of clothes," he says with an impish smile.

This season Jiovanni had to ask a more experienced roommate for instructions. He got laughed at and called a "youngin'" and "rookie boy," but, he says, "I definitely know how to do laundry now."

The youngest of three boys, Jiovanni is a tall, thin, easygoing California kid who still seems a little surprised by his good fortune. And fortune is what it is. As a first-round and twenty-first-overall draft pick, Jiovanni got a $1.358 million signing bonus from the Houston Astros out of high school in 2009.

At the Legends he is paid $1,100 a month. Sixty of that goes to the clubhouse manager, or clubbie, who washes his uniform and otherwise takes care of the clubhouse where the players hang out. On the road he and his teammates get $20 a day in meal money and whatever pregame snack the visiting team is offering. "The place we came [from], it was peanut butter sandwiches, that's it," he says. "Other places we got good croissant sandwiches and hot dogs and stuff, so it varies." At home tonight at Applebee's Park it was peanut butter and jelly sandwiches and potato salad. After the game ends around ten or eleven tonight, they will get whatever is open, "fast food, Applebee's, that's pretty much it," says Jiovanni. "It sucks."

Especially for a kid who loves to eat. In phone calls home to his mother he gets instructions on how to cook eggs, omelets, and grilled cheese sandwiches. His family knows how much he misses home-cooked meals, so they take pictures of what they cook and send them to him. They mean well. Almost all the girls in the extended family play softball and the boys baseball, but Jio has made it further than anyone, and they are proud of him, said his mother. At a big game when Jio was still in high school, about a hundred family members came to cheer him on. They wore T-shirts on which they had written things like "Go Jio" and "Hit me a home run Jio."

In the condo he shares with three other players are whatever dishes their mothers have left behind after visiting. Jiovanni has been living away from his parents about a year and is still getting used to certain things—like doing laundry—that older players tease he would have mastered if he had gone to college. And that is what he had planned to do. He had even signed a letter of intent to play at the University of Southern California. But a $1.358 million signing bonus is hard to turn down. So his first time living on his own was last summer when he was playing in Greenville. "I'm still kind of adjusting to it, just being away from my family and my parents, but it definitely makes you grow up and kind of mature on your own," he says.

Like many mothers, his isn't quite ready to let go. Jio may be a six-foot-two professional athlete, but before the start of the season Leticia took him to the Broadway musical *The Lion King*, to remind him of the animated movie he loved as a little boy.

Jose was seventeen when he left Venezuela to play professional baseball in the United States. He signed as a nondrafted free agent for $20,000. At the time, he says, "I thought it was good, but now I realize." He doesn't need to finish: $20,000 to a seventeen-year-old living in Venezuela looks a lot different than it does to a twenty-year-old who has been playing professional baseball in the United States for three years.

Jose's height, or lack of it, is a favorite topic among sportswriters. Jose tells them he wants to prove that small people can play in the big leagues. People may question his size, he says, but on the field he feels the same as everybody. Legends batting coach Stubby Clapp describes him as a high-energy acrobatic player, a "spark plug."

That explosive energy coupled with his matching dimples make him a fan favorite almost everywhere he goes. In Greenville it was reported that his photo was even used on team billboards. But when he first started playing professional baseball in the United States, Jose was even more clueless than Jiovanni. Not only did he not know how to do laundry; he didn't know how to speak the language. He has worked hard on his English and is now one of the better English-speaking Latin players on the team, says Jiovanni. When Jose stumbles on a word, Jiovanni, the son of Mexican immigrants, helps out.

Jio grew up hearing stories about how his grandfather played baseball in Mexico without cleats and sometimes without a glove. When he was a teenager he visited Mexico City, where both his parents were born. Like many children of immigrants, he didn't get away with much growing up, said his mother. No practice or playing until his homework was done. He may have been the little big brother, because of his height, but he had older brothers to answer to. And he still does.

Jose and the Latin players he lives with are on their own. It is too far and too difficult for any of their families to visit. When the season ends they will return to their families, living six months in Latin America and the other six months in the

United States. The common thread is baseball, which most of them play year round, going from the season in the United States to winter league in their home countries.

At the end of last season Jiovanni played some instructional league and then spent the rest of the time home in Southern California with his family. This season he has sought advice from his brother, Jessie, who plays for the AA Chattanooga Lookouts in Tennessee. He is hoping he may even be able to visit Jessie this year. It is only a three-hour drive, and when you are in one of the worst travel leagues in the Minors and your shortest bus ride is five hours, then three hours doesn't seem bad.

As buses go, though, both Jiovanni and Jose are pretty happy with the leather reclining chairs and Internet access theirs offers. The latter is especially important, because the movies on offer are pretty bad, says Jose, who prefers to watch his own movies on his laptop.

Jose has been pleased with his season so far, but Jiovanni is having a little more trouble. The team itself, which plays in the South Atlantic League, started out strong, winning their home opener and thus saving Alan's mustache. The rest of April they seemed to trade wins and losses and did about the same in May. Jiovanni had a dismal batting average in both April and May, .203 and .212, respectively. He doesn't feel he is doing as well as he is capable of doing, but is quick to add that he is learning a lot and growing, especially when it comes to his mental game. Early in the season he was questioning his confidence, but after talking with the coach he realized he has a better mental attitude toward hitting and playing in general, he says. One thing that helps is when he gets too frustrated, he reminds himself this is what he wants to do. "I chose to do this," he says. "I'll probably never grow out of the game. I see myself doing this for a long time."

A few minutes later, as Jiovanni, Jose, and their teammates warm up, little boys in baby-blue Cubs gear and little girls in red softball uniforms swarm the dugout. Parents armed with cameras and camcorders block the entrance, fanning out only when their children take the field with the ballplayers. A few children stand by each player as Miss Teen America 2010, who happens to be from nearby Cynthiana, Kentucky, belts out the national anthem.

Little Dorsey Franklin in the sailor outfit wasn't chosen to sing the anthem this season. "We were surprised, but at the same time we weren't," said her mother, Lucille. They planned to try again the following year and even were sent an invitation by the Legends, but in the end forgot. Dorsey kept busy; she was a finalist in the 2010 Kentucky State Fair Children's Talent Division as well as a winner of the 2010 Tennessee State Fair in the Children's Talent Division. By 2011 she was flying to Florida for work.

The Beaumont Quartet was chosen for the third year in a row. The Legends went on to win the game at which the quartet performed, leading Frieda Gebert to declare, "They should make us a tradition because they win every time we sing." Unfortunately, the tradition would be broken in 2011, when tryouts were held during a week when one of the quartet members was out of town.

•

But back to 2010, before the children took the field, a parade of pooches walked with their owners from third base to first as part of the night's "Bark in the Park" promotion. After the kids and pets are finished, the game against the Delmarva Shorebirds of Salisbury, Maryland, gets under way. In the bottom of the first, when Jose steps up to bat, Jiovanni pats him on the back. They are batting first and second, and both are out almost immediately.

An inning or two later, Charley Irons makes his way through the crowds of double-fisted beer-holding fans and up to the press box. The name on the back of his blue PNC Bank T-shirt reads Harry. And tonight that is who he is, Harry, the guy who wears the black wig, huge straw sombrero, or both, and updates scores by hand on a large PNC board out in left field. The Legends' scoreboard is automated, but Harry's job is not.

Not many teams still employ the equivalent of a Harry, but the stadium was designed to be reminiscent of old ball parks like Wrigley and Crosley Fields. None of this concerns Charley. He is hustling to get the scores. He can get the two Major League scores he posts—the parent Astros and nearby Cincinnati Reds—sent to him as text updates on his phone. But he has to come inside, to the press box on the second floor of the park, for the Minor League scores he posts, which include all the teams in the South Atlantic League in which the Legends play.

The guy in the press box who usually gives him the scores isn't here tonight, and at first Charley has a little trouble finding someone else who will help him. A thin teenager in knee-high yellow socks and old-school baseball pants that end below his knee, Charley looks even younger than his eighteen years. He is hesitant to interrupt any of the three men sitting at computers by the long window overlooking the field. Finally, a man in the corner helps him out, looking the scores up on the Internet and writing them on a slip of paper for Charley.

With the paper in his hand, Charley walks back down onto the main concourse, braves the beer-swigging fans, and exits the field. Outside, behind left field, he sifts through an old shed filled with binder paper–size metal number plates. He pulls out a few zeros, a one, and a three and places them on top of the shed. He checks the paper on which the scores are written and then pulls out some more numbers, the slightly larger ones for the score, the smaller ones for the inning.

Once he has all the numerals he needs, he shuts the shed and places his stack of numbers on the walkway in front of the PNC board before climbing a steep ladder up there himself. He is now at about the same level as the raised bleachers one hundred feet or so away in left field. Out here there are a few things to watch out for, including the flames that shoot out of two stacks on the main Legends scoreboard during big innings. "They're really loud so you'll jump," he explains. "I've seen outfielders jump." He's also heard them swear, on bad plays, but insists he has never heard Legends players swear, just visiting teams.

Alan tries to keep their image clean. When he learns that all of the Latin players are crammed into a single condo, you can sense he is going to try to do something about that. When I first approached him about following the team, he asked if I was going to write a positive or negative book. I said I would write what I saw, but I wouldn't hide anything. Alan agreed that was fair. He knew the players wouldn't let me see anything that would jeopardize their futures. Many have agents. They have been hounded by the media since they were kids, and they know how to act. They are neither choir boys nor renegades, but until they are so washed up their futures don't matter, they keep their flaws hidden.

•

On good plays, when Charley operates the scoreboard and congratulates the outfielders, they usually say thanks. It is as close as he gets to a conversation when he is Harry. He updates the scores only twice a night. The rest of the time he simply sits or stands out here watching the game. It doesn't take him long to slide in the new scores. A few of the top numbers require a little acrobatics, balancing on the gate in front of his walkway with one foot and pushing against the PNC board with the other as he reaches to slide in the top number on the board. But the lower ones he can do simply by standing on the walkway and reaching up.

In the fall he will head to the University of Alabama to study finance. This is his summer job, and as summer jobs go, it isn't bad. Especially when compared to his previous experience in the fast-food industry. "I used to work for Chick-fil-A two summers ago," he says. "Chick-fil-A has ups and downs, like free meals are good, but overall I like this job a lot better."

His job is more than just being Harry. He is part of the Legends promotion team, a group of several dozen young people who alternate in roles like Harry and on the Mac Attack beat. The latter basically involves entertaining the crowds with gimmicks, games, and cheers between innings. It is less lonely but more stressful, especially if the sponsor of that particular giveaway or gimmick is present.

Charley is comfortable in front of a crowd, and making fun of himself, so the Mac Attack, which requires one to wear McDonald's bright-red and yellow shorts and shirts is a fun job for him. He doesn't even mind being asked to get in costume as a guest mascot or other character. Tonight Scooby Doo, who is making a special appearance for Bark in the Park, isn't quite so pleased. The rumor is he got roped into the role after calling in at the last minute to say he couldn't work a game during the last home stretch.

As Harry tonight, Charley is wearing the sombrero, which so far this summer has proved more popular than the wig. Both headpieces and the Harry T-shirt are a bit of a mystery to Charley. "I'm new this year. I don't know the whole tradition behind it," he says. "I just go with the flow."

He doesn't bring a book or magazine out here and refrains from texting or talking on his cell phone out of respect for his position. When children sitting in the bleachers across from him give him a shout, he answers back. Usually they just want him to promise to give them a ball if he catches one. It doesn't look like there is much chance of that tonight. He didn't even bring out the glove they keep in the promotions room for just such an occasion. All he has with him is his phone and a bottle of water.

Now that the numbers are updated, there is nothing left to do but watch the game, which Lexington is losing 4–1 in the fourth inning. Spending so much time at a baseball field, he has come to understand just how important it is to watch the game, especially the ball. The worst thing he's ever seen is when a man took a line-drive hit to the face. He didn't actually see it, but he saw the aftermath with emergency medical workers and a twenty-minute game delay. "I don't like gore, but I heard there was like blood in a five-seat radius," he says.

When he was on Mac Attack one night, he was hanging out by the visiting team's bullpen and heard not a single word of English. All the players were speaking Spanish, which, he says, shows you how the Minor Leagues are changing, especially at the Class-A level. The parent organization drafts or signs a lot of people from places like Cuba, Venezuela, and the Dominican Republic, and they'll come into the organization like raw projects, he explains. "I guess the best way to say it is they get stuck in Single-A forever, or for a long time," he says.

American players like Jiovanni, who come straight out of high school, can also end up in Class-A for a longer stretch, he says, but players who have played some college ball seem to move up more quickly. While he believes the team's best hitters this season are J. D. Martinez and Kody Hinze, his favorite defensive player is Grant Hogue, who plays center field. From his perch on the PNC walkway, Charley can hear Grant barking out the tendencies of certain hitters, almost like a "quarterback of the outfield."

Charley may love sports, but the roles he gets to play are less romantic. Every night someone on the promotions team is designated the "fat lady." At the end of the night, if the Legends win, the fat lady gets sent out on the field to sing. Whoever is the fat lady dresses in a fat-lady costume, complete with a Viking-type headpiece with horns and long blonde braids. Charley has performed the role three or four times but is not her tonight. The Harry usually does not get assigned the fat-lady role.

They play the music, but they turn it on really low, he says, "so everybody can hear your awful voice." They don't sing the whole song, just a few lines, which Charley offers up now in a flat voice: "Celebrate good times. Come on." He continues, "I usually do it in the highest-pitched voice I can. It sounds horrible. I usually get booed off the field."

Once he almost didn't even make it to the field. It was his first time doing the fat lady. It was the top of the ninth, the game was almost over, and he was dressed and ready and thought he had better head out to the field. But another member of the staff spotted him, grabbed him, and put him back in the promotions room. Then he told Charley about the superstition that if the fat lady comes out before the game is completely over, the Legends will lose, no matter the circumstances. Charley has never brought the fat lady out early again.

3. A Loyal Following

This is what Legends president Alan Stein doesn't want you to see. Nine Latin players crammed into a two-bedroom condo. Air mattresses occupy every free space, sometimes with players still sleeping on them. Three days' worth of trash is stuffed in several large trash bags in the kitchen, sheets hang from the windows, and furniture is limited to egg crates and a folding table. In the morning the line for the shower stretches down the hall.

The place looks like a temporary crash pad. And that is after shortstop Jiovanni Mier warned second baseman Jose Altuve that visitors were coming. Jio's place feels a little more like a home, or at least a fraternity house. Sheets still serve as curtains, shower curtains as doors, and the edge of the kitchen counter as a hook for hanging clothes, but there are real beds here—and only four players.

Each player has his own room, two with real walls and two

created by hanging shower curtains from the ceiling. Jiovanni has a room with walls on the third floor, which the air-conditioning has trouble reaching. He rents the bed, bedside table, dresser, and, in a way, the television, a thirty-two-inch flat screen from Wal-Mart, with its edges still encased in protective plastic. Wal-Mart has a money-back return policy if you return the television in ninety days. So Jiovanni will return this television after eighty days or so and then go to another Wal-Mart and buy another television he will keep another eighty days or so before returning it as well. It's what a lot of baseball players do, he says.

Not all his purchases have been so stingy. Parked outside is what his girlfriend refers to as his baby, a shiny white Chevy Tahoe with custom wheels. A large signing bonus in the hands of a teenager is like giving a little kid a five-dollar bill in a candy store, said Jio's mother, Leticia. For the most part, though, Jio is pretty grounded about his money, she said. He purchased the television, lamp, and the sheets that serve as curtains during his girlfriend Kristen Lawson's first visit to Lexington earlier in the season. "We went to Wal-Mart. It was, like, one in the morning after a game," says Jiovanni.

They also did a lot of laundry, the kind of romantic stuff a nineteen-year-old former cheerleader flies across the country to do. Before Jiovanni became a professional baseball player, Kristen had never flown alone. Now she flies to a lot of places she never thought she would visit—like Kentucky.

She hails from Southern California and is pretty in a laid-back West Coast way, with long blonde hair and clear skin. It is late June, and she arrived in town earlier in the week to spend the three-day All-Star break with her boyfriend. He wasn't selected to play in the South Atlantic League's All-Star Game, a baseball midsummer classic in which top players from the league's fourteen teams face off in a game. It's no surprise, really. Although his batting average improved in June to .256, it was still nothing to brag about. Overall the team is faring better, however, with 10 wins and 8 losses so far in June.

But for Jio it's been a hard year. He won't say it, but those close to him maintain that family and faith have helped him get through what is turning out to be a very disappointing season. If he isn't talking to his mother, he's talking to his father or one of his two older brothers. Engraved on his bat and on his iPod he has Bible verses, reminding him such things as "with God all things are possible."

The possibilities of what to do in Lexington when he isn't playing baseball are more limited. Kristen has been here before, but aside from the ballpark, Jiovanni's apartment, and the fast-food restaurants they frequent, she hasn't seen much of the city. "We woke up yesterday thinking, instead of just waking up, having lunch, me going to the field, let's wake up early and do something," says Jiovanni. "And we woke up, were just like, 'What are we going to do?' We just went, got food, and came right back."

Tonight they do have plans. Kristen wants to stay for the postgame fireworks so they can have their own Fourth of July, a holiday they won't be spending together. Although they have been dating since high school, they don't really consider themselves high school sweethearts, because it wasn't until the end of their senior year that they got together. Back then Kristen thought Jiovanni would be going to the University of Southern California, where he had been offered a full ride. Then he was drafted, on graduation day. "It was one of those dramatic moments where he was, like, late to graduation, ran in like on a movie," she says.

Kristen learned that Jiovanni had been drafted while she was in the gym getting ready with their classmates before graduation. Jiovanni didn't show up until after everyone was seated, and then he ran in. He has been running around the Minor Leagues ever since. While she is staying near home to attend a junior college and work at a frozen-yogurt store, he has been traveling through small towns in the middle of the country she never thought she would see, like Greenville, Tennessee, and Lexington, Kentucky.

Before she started dating Jiovanni, she wasn't really into baseball. Jiovanni teases her for her lack of athleticism and sports knowledge. When a fly ball bounced slowly toward her in the stands one day, she ducked instead of leaning down to catch it. More troubling as far as Jio is concerned is what could have happened at the previous day's game. Kristen was sitting near home plate, in an area without netting where Jiovanni had seen a guy take a ball to the face earlier. From the dugout he kept motioning to her to move, but she didn't get what he was trying to say. Finally, the girl she was sitting with figured it out, and they moved.

When Kristen isn't visiting, Jiovanni usually sleeps until late morning, but because her time with him is limited, they got up early this day and by noon had already grabbed lunch at Subway. The food in the house is limited to large containers of peanut butter, beer, and a freezer full of casserole dishes left by visiting mothers. There are a few pots purchased by Jiovanni's mother during her last visit, but they don't get used much. After games Jiovanni and his roommates usually head to whatever is open—Applebee's, Subway, Qdoba. Before games they do the same. Eating at home happens only when mothers are visiting or the casserole dishes they leave behind are being devoured. Occasionally, they keep milk and other perishables in the refrigerator. But it's hard because they have to finish the food before heading on the road, or it will go bad while they are gone for ten-day stretches. Jio will end up losing quite a bit of weight during the season, which some will theorize played a factor in his less than stellar performance.

The whole team rents condos in the same complex near a chain electronics store and about a five-minute drive from the ballpark. But only one condo of players seems to actually cook. That's the Latin house, so named because it is where all the Latin players live.

It is a few doors down from Jiovanni's place and a world away. Jose stays in an upstairs room, one of only two residents in the condo who sleeps on a real bed. He upgraded after his air mattress exploded one night. Then he convinced his roommate to do the same.

There is no cable or even television here, unless you count the bulky old thing sitting in the kitchen that doesn't work. But there are a folding table, pots and pans, and food. In this house they cook, explains Jose, "Rice, chicken, rice, rice."

How exactly they get their groceries is a bit of a mystery, because none of them has a car, and only a few, Jose included, really speak English. They have friends, though, Javier and Pri, who help out. They don't know their friends' last names, or much about them, except that they are Latin and available to take them to get groceries and deal with other aspects of daily life, like delivering the rent. In this house they are the equivalent of the visiting mothers. No real mothers ever make it this far. Jose doesn't even keep any photos of his family here because it just makes him miss them more. He does keep a Batman blanket a girl back home gave him, but the girl is no longer in the picture. Before he left, his younger brother gave him a rosary that he wears every game. He keeps in touch with everyone back home on Facebook and otherwise passes the time off the field watching videos on his laptop and listening to music. He's into vampires and the underworld.

Not long ago he celebrated his twentieth birthday. A few streamers and deflated balloons still hang from the wall above his bed. Although he just returned from the All-Star Game, he isn't happy with how he is hitting. He wants to be hitting .300, not .280, and although he didn't have a break like most of the other guys, he insists he isn't tired. "No, we still have sixty-eight more games," he says. "I don't have to be tired."

But he does have to be ready. It is close to one o'clock, time for him and the other Latin players to go outside and wait for rides to the ballpark. It's an understood agreement, and no Latin player has ever missed a game for lack of a ride. One or two guys did miss a ride, says Jose, but they made it to the field before the game started. So he changes and heads downstairs and out the door.

Outside a truck pulls up, and Jose and two other guys head toward it, the last guy limping as fast as he can toward the waiting vehicle. Next Jiovanni pulls out in his sparkly Chevy Tahoe. He takes another four Latin guys, who magically exit their condo door just as he is driving by. As soon as that load of players is gone, another player leaves the Latin house, sits down on the front stoop, and waits a few minutes. After a while he gets up, heads down the street, and calls back over his shoulder to the last guy in the house. And then, before you know it, they are all gone.

●

At the field, as the players are getting ready for the game, Chris Pearl is taking a break. When the team is home he usually arrives at the ballpark around nine in the morning and doesn't leave until an hour or so after the game ends, which is usually about eleven at night. It is a rough life during the season, but being head groundskeeper suits Chris and his nine-year-old son, Zachary, a.k.a. "Mini Pearl," perfectly.

Chris started in the grounds business while still in high school. Back then he worked on golf courses, but now it's baseball fields. Either way it's an outdoor job for which he's well suited. "I was a hyperactive kid. I have a hyperactive kid. I love being outside," he says, sitting at a shaded picnic table near the park's concession stands.

When he first started out in the golf course business, his job wasn't year-round and he had to work inside during the winter, bagging groceries or in a warehouse. It drove him stir crazy. Now his job is year-round, albeit quite a bit lighter during the winter and very busy in summer, but year-round all the same. He switched sports while still living in nearby Louisville, where he grew up. It was after the AAA Louisville Bats had built their new stadium a decade ago that he got into the baseball business. He wasn't the head groundskeeper there, but he was on the crew, and after another stop he learned the ropes enough to move his way all the way up to the Majors. He was on the Houston Astros' crew when the team went to the World Series in 2005, and just like the players, he has a ring to prove it.

Now he is in charge, but back in Class-A. It was an easy choice. Chris wanted to be closer to his son, who lives in Louisville with Chris's ex. In summer Mini Pearl, who lives about ninety miles away, spends a lot of time with his father at the park. He has free rein and likes to hang out by the huge inflatable children's toys when they are being blown up, with a woman who serves food in the suites when he is hungry, and with his father, when Chris drags the field in the fourth and seventh innings. The dirt is the hardest part of the job for Chris. It isn't really dirt, though. "It's called dirt, but technically there's no 'dirt' in it," he explains. "It's 40 percent clay . . . and 40 percent sand, and the other 20 percent is silt."

It is delivered by truckload from Alabama, and the players have very specific instructions about how it should feel. They want their spikes to be able to sink into it without effort, but not to leave a footprint. It's a very fine line that is aided by adding just enough water.

It is early afternoon, and the dirt has already been watered three times today for a total of two hours. This is done in an effort to get the moisture to settle down into the six-inch-deep dirt. How much water to deliver is something Chris has learned from experience. It also depends on the weather. Too much water and the dirt turns slimy and superslick, which is why when it rains the tarp goes on to cover the field. The saying in baseball goes that four tons of this valuable dirt disappear from an infield each year, taken away by the wind, transferred to players' clothes when they slide, and mud clumps that stick to their spikes. Chris is in his fourth season with the Legends and so far has added twenty-five to thirty tons of new dirt.

Then there is the grass, which, this being Kentucky, is blue-grass. Bluegrass is a cool-season grass, which means it grows better when the temperature is in the seventies during the day, not the nineties, like it tends to hit around here in summer. A lot of ballparks in the South use warm-season grass, which grows better in warmer weather and can be mowed a lot shorter, a half inch to three-quarters of an inch versus the inch and a quarter Chris keeps the bluegrass. It doesn't sound like a lot, but when you're talking grass, and the speed the ball gets to you, it really is a big difference, says Chris. Another difference is the price.

Bluegrass ends up costing more because it needs more water in the hot weather and is more prone to disease. "Grass is a living, breathing organism, and when it is stressed out, it gets diseased," explains Chris.

Most of that stress is induced by its getting wet, really hot, or really humid. Even when the team is away, the grass isn't resting, due to concerts and other bookings, making Chris's job even more challenging. The previous week the state high school baseball tournament was held here. With dozens of games over four days, there was no time for Chris to water the way he normally does, and that, coupled with the high temperatures, caused disease to break out. In the past two weeks he has spent thirteen hundred dollars on fungicide to keep fungus from growing. When he was younger he might have been annoyed with the extra events. At thirty-eight, he views them in a different light—as job security. "They tear it up, make it look bad," he says. It's a "feather in my cap if I can get it back to where it needs to be in quick time and as cost-effective as possible."

The weather also keeps him on his toes. If there is a 30 percent or greater chance of rain when the team is home, he puts the tarp over the field after games. On game days he also decides if the weather looks like it will be bad enough to merit getting out the tarp—that is, until the umpires and managers meet, at which point it is up to the umpires. But because at this level many of them are young and inexperienced, Chris tends to approach them between half innings if he thinks the tarp should go on. Once it is on, it must stay for forty-five minutes before the game is called or the tarp is removed. Those are the rules.

Most of Chris's real work is done in the morning. That is when he waters, mows, and gets things in order. Once the team starts batting practice, he can't mess with the field much, but he usually sticks around for a while to make sure things are going okay and the players aren't getting any crazy hops. "That's basically what all those guys live or die by," he explains, "whether the ball comes to them smoothly and it's not bouncing around everywhere, with them having to worry about one bouncing up and hitting them in the face."

If he doesn't maintain the field properly, it can get bumps and humps. That is when groundskeepers worry about players complaining that they had three balls come to them with each one acting differently. One may have stayed down where it should be, another might have had a crazy hop to the right, and the third might have bounced over their head. All of which boils down to his main goal: to provide a safe field. If he can make it look nice as well, that's great, but his priority is to make sure it is safe. "Because there are guys out there that are millionaires," says Chris. "And if you got a field that's got a bunch of holes in it, they go out there, tear a knee up or something like that, you could cost the organization a lot of money." And cost the player a career. So Chris stays busy making sure that doesn't happen. After the visiting Rome Braves of Rome, Georgia, finish batting practice, he zooms out on a Gator utility vehicle, his son by his side. With his staff he pulls away the batting-practice equipment. Then they rake, pound, and water the dirt before zooming off again so the game can get started.

Chris's conscientiousness is not uncommon among Legends employees. It is difficult not to give it your all around Alan, said his friend Billy Forbess. That is because everybody knows that Alan will do everything he can to make it all work and never asks anybody to do nearly as much as he does himself. Take the time entertainer Myron Noodleman missed a scheduled Legends game-day appearance due to a canceled flight. Myron's nerdy dance is no easy act to take on, but Alan bought a tuxedo and dressed up as Noodleman, said Billy. "He got out on the field and did the Noodleman stuff rather than disappointing the fans."

Tonight he is leaving the entertaining to the professionals. In his office, not far from the park's main entrance, Alan and his wife, Kathy, watch the opening show on television. After a local man killed while fighting in the Middle East is honored, Alan turns to his wife to confirm that the flag that flashed across the screen was at half-mast. She is pretty sure it was. As chief operating officer of a company that oversees more teams than just the Legends, Alan isn't supposed to get too bogged down in the little details, but Legends manager Andy Shea said Alan still cares about them. He always makes sure there are picture frames for photos taken of those who throw out the first pitch and bunting around the stadium, minor routine stuff like that, said Andy. "I don't think he could ever stand to be just a guy that looks at my sales reports and game-day reports and be the guy who judges on that," said Andy. "I could just never picture him not listening to the entire radio broadcast when we're on the road to see what Keith [the team broadcaster] is talking about and see what order advertisers' spots were played."

Which is why Alan is in his office now watching his television, which shows the feed to MiLB.TV, checking out the ceremonial first pitches, listening to the national anthem, and otherwise making sure he is aware of everything that's going on. From the cupolas on the stadium, reminiscent of nearby horse farms, to the stadium's location on the north side of Lexington and the team's name, it all has Alan's mark. He brags he sketched the design for the stadium on a napkin over drinks at a restaurant one night.

The location was a little harder. When he realized the city wasn't going to help, his dream of an urban ballpark died. Downtown property was too expensive without city backing, plus the city owned much of it, and he sure wasn't going to buy downtown property from the city after it had refused to help fund the project. So he started looking elsewhere. One of the places he looked was the north side of town, close to the downtown core, the thoroughfare, and the grittier side of things. One of his top choices was the small shopping mall where the ballpark now resides, but for a long time the family that had inherited the land wasn't interested. Then Alan met them face-to-face and told them about baseball. "And I talked to them about the magic and the poetry and the romance of baseball," he said. "And after about ten minutes, fifteen minutes, one of the daughters said to the mother, 'Mom, remember when Dad used to take us up to Reds games at Crosley Field on the train? How much fun that was? He really loved baseball, didn't he?'" And that was it; they decided to sell then and there. Alan was about two hundred thousand dollars short, so he offered them a thirty thousand dollar-a-year suite for ten years. They accepted and never used it.

Other things have been easier, like the naming of the team. Alan wanted the name to be an alliteration. They conducted several focus groups, asked for public input, and allowed the public to vote, having done enough research and enough skewing to know the name they wanted would win. Then, at a press conference, a reporter asked about Horse Flies, a name Alan thought was funny, but one he didn't think stood a chance. For kicks, Alan decided to announce that, while the Legends name was in first place, Horse Flies was in twentieth. "And it hit the news, and within the next day there were like five thousand votes for Horse Flies. It almost caught up," he said. "It scared me to death." Well, not really, he admits, because it wouldn't have mattered. They were still going to name the team the Lexington

Legends. But Horse Flies ended up second, and Alan has been a little more careful with his public statements ever since. It hasn't stopped him from joking around, though. He does plenty of that.

A few of the guys on staff have a bet each night about how long the national anthem will last and use a stopwatch to time it. They have three seconds after the performance starts to place their bets. The winner gets five dollars and bragging rights. When he is on the field Alan claims he usually wins. Having listened to thousands of national anthem tryouts every year, he is a bit of an expert. He admits, though, that even he can get fooled. Take the girl last night. "She was about on pace for 1:34, which is relatively slow. Then, at the very end, she just stopped and ended up at 1:55," he says. The average is between 1:18 and 1:25. The longest in Legends history was 5:24, performed by a blind woman with a soulful gospel style who kept repeating herself. The shortest was around 34 seconds, presented by a grade school group that got off and running and never slowed down.

Kind of like Alan. Ten years in he is still doing the same crazy stunts. Luckily, this year he didn't have to shave his mustache. His wife is happy about that. She sits in his office in khaki shorts and a polo shirt, her blonde hair in a neat bob. The local media consider Kathy her husband's equal and just as colorful a character. She is an unabashed liberal with two pit bulls named Ike and Tina. Kathy hasn't been at the ballpark as much as usual this year because there was a special legislative session. The first few years she came all the time.

The very first year there was a player, an eighteen-year-old pitcher, who was almost a part of the Stein family. He came to dinner, worked with one of their sons on his baseball, and taught Kathy a lot about the life of a Minor League player. From him she learned how day to day their existence is, how they never know what is going to happen, the unpredictability of it all. That player is no longer in the game. When he was promoted to AA, he ended up needing Tommy John surgery and never recovered. Now he is a card dealer in Las Vegas like his father. Alan tried to track him down last time he was there, but never found him.

There are other things Kathy has learned from the sport, some of which she uses in politics, a passion she says she inherited from her forebears. In her family, the women always ran the campaigns and the men ran the races. Back then they were Republicans. Kathy is a Democrat, but the principles, she maintains, are the same; the party is what changed, she says, not her.

In a state where sex education until recently largely consisted of abstinence only, she has championed scientific-based sex education. She supports the legalization of marijuana and has stood up against legislation requiring pregnant woman to view ultrasounds prior to their abortions and Bible study in schools. Her husband calls her the Richard Nixon of Kentucky politics. "There aren't many people who are ambivalent" about Kathy, says Alan. "Plenty of people who think she's the devil, plenty, and a similar number who think she's the most courageous, incredible advocate in Kentucky politics."

In her husband's office she comes across as a polite southern wife, petite, blonde, and saying nothing outrageous. Occasionally, she merges her husband's passion with her work as a Kentucky state senator. "Baseball is such a romantic, quote-filled, story-filled endeavor since its beginning that I'm able to draw upon that from time to time in floor speeches and questions, or whatever," she says.

But even romance can suffer when the economy is not doing well, and the Great Recession has impacted the Legends. The past two years have been extraordinarily difficult. The business is not recession proof, but because it is an inexpensive family-orientated entertainment option, it is a little bit recession resistant. In Alan's opinion entertainment is one of the last things people give up. But other aspects of the business are harder to maintain, like sponsorships and advertisers, which people are not currently making commitments to for a full season. Alan remains fully committed. He tries to answer personally every e-mail he receives, an average of about three hundred a day. "He is very engaged with those people personally. That's one reason he has been so successful," said his friend Billy Forbess. "He is truly interested in the fans. Besides just so they buy the tickets, he's interested in them as people, as human beings."

He may know Warren Buffet personally (they have shared ownership of another team), but Alan treats fans as if they are just as important to him. And in a way they are. He knows that without them he wouldn't be here. So during games he seldom sits in his seat, instead greeting them individually. "For ten years Alan has treated this as kind of his own private cocktail party," says Kathy. He greets people as they come in, he goes around to the various suites, and he stands at the gates as they exit.

Tonight, after stopping by her husband's office, Kathy heads to their seats. Alan leaves his office at the top of the second inning, but it is the bottom of the third before he finally takes his seat next to his wife. First he shakes a few hands, says hi to an older woman, and then sits down to chat with a scout. After talking with the scout, he greets an usher who updates him on a situation involving broken seats. Then he makes his way to his seat, shaking a few more hands on the way. He slouches back for a minute before the Legends hit a home run, and then he is on his feet, Kathy at his side, dancing a little dance.

4. Past Legends and Future Stars

Jose is no longer a Legend. He is a JetHawk. He was assigned to the Class-A (advanced) Lancaster JetHawks at the end of July. In his ninety-four Legends games, Jose had 11 home runs, 39 stolen bases, and 45 runs batted in and batted .308. He will go on to spend the off-season playing with Major League players in the Venezuelan professional league. He will play so well there will be expectations that he will be moved up to AA for the 2011 season. But that is yet to come. Right now the Legends' former spark plug is setting things alight in Lancaster, California.

Freddy Acevedo never made it out of Lexington. His last season with the Legends was in 2004. He is twenty-nine, a husband, father, and baseball coach. And he still misses his playing days, misses every aspect of being a professional baseball player—taking batting practice, making a diving catch in the outfield, getting ready to take the infield, the feeling when you hit the ball in the right spot and know it's gone and nobody is going to catch it.

He plays amateur baseball now. His teammates are older, less competitive, and don't necessarily play the game the right way. Freddy runs to take the outfield; he runs to take the infield. Everyone else walks. "I don't think that anybody who has played the game, and loved the game, can ever say when they stop playing that they're gonna be at peace when they're not playing," he says.

At first he found it hard to watch the Legends because he missed playing so much, but now he just finds it hard to fit them in. With a two-year-old son and a full-time job, there isn't much time left to watch three-hour baseball games. He has been to two Legends games this season and won't be staying for tonight's.

Freddy is here this afternoon for only a brief visit and will be gone long before first pitch. Every once in a while as he watches from the stands he waves at a player warming up on the field or greets a member of the front-office staff. But mostly he keeps to himself.

Dressed in jeans and a T-shirt, the only reminders of his playing days are the "what ifs" that haunt him when he looks out at the field. What if he had done this, what if somebody had told him not to do that, what if? There are so many. But as he tells his baseball story, laughter cuts through the sadness.

It begins in the Dominican Republic, where he played on the streets with a broomstick for a bat and the heads of his sisters' dolls for balls. When he was six years old his father took him to an organized team and gave him the choice of playing baseball or getting a job. Freddy chose baseball.

His own father hadn't had that option. Freddy's grandfather worked as a supervisor in the sugar-cane fields, and as a child his father had to help the family by shining shoes and performing other odd jobs.

Freddy was faced with different opportunities. When he was sixteen his coach took him to the big league teams' nearby academies so they could get a look at him. Two teams were interested, but only one, the Astros, was willing to wait to sign him until he finished high school. He was seventeen and received a $17,500 signing bonus. After graduating from high school in 1999 he spent the summer at the Astros' Dominican academy just thirty minutes from his home.

He went home on weekends, an experience he compares to college, an opportunity he never had the chance to pursue. Not many ballplayers from his country do; they get signed as teenagers, leave school early, and live in fear once they make it to the United States that they will be released. They don't know how to do anything but play baseball, and if that is taken from them, they are lost.

Freddy at least finished high school and thanks to his parents' insistence studied some English. He thought he knew the language pretty well. He knew everything they taught at the academy where he spent two years before being sent to Florida for spring training in March 2001. It was at a Hardee's restaurant in Florida that he learned otherwise. Freddy went up to the counter to place his order. The man on the other side started talking. To Freddy it sounded like "Blah, blah, blah." He said yes. Then the guy started talking again, "Blah, blah, blah." Freddy said yes again. It happened once more, and Freddy said yes one more time. Then the man told him his total—$19.99. Freddy was trying to figure out what he had ordered when the guy came back with four or five burgers, the same number of drinks, and quite a few french fries. That's how Freddy learned he had ordered the special.

He decided he needed to improve his English, and when he

was sent to Rookie League in Martinsville, Virginia, he started hanging out with the American players, listening to their accents and use of slang. He also listened to a lot of pop music: Britney Spears, Christina Aguilera, *N-SYNC, and the Backstreet Boys. Rap music was too fast, country was unintelligible, but pop music was perfect. He would download the lyrics from the Internet and then listen to the music while reading the lyrics.

Language wasn't the only thing he had to master off the field. In Martinsville it became clear pretty quickly that none of the Latin players Freddy lived with knew how to cook. His first clue was the rice a Venezuelan player made. It was soupy. Freddy tried the chicken. It was bloody. So he called his mother and spent an hour and a half on the phone getting recipes. Then he became the official cook at the Latin house.

Although he liked to practice English with his American teammates, it was with his Latin teammates that Freddy developed the closest ties. The American players had cell phones and families. The Latin players had calling cards and each other. The Americans had cars and an understanding of how things worked in their country. The Latin players had air mattresses and each other. They acted like brothers because they didn't have anybody else. None of them had cars, and in Martinsville they would wait for the trainer to take them to the ballpark. In Lexington they would wait near the entrance to the complex where all the players lived for their American teammates to drive by. But a lot of the American players did just that, drive by. A few would stop, but not enough, so some of the Latin players would have to take a cab to the ballpark.

Then one day hardly any cars drove by. The Latin players figured the Americans were leaving earlier, so the next day they went out to wait even earlier. But still, only one or two American players drove by. They figured out there was another exit, and the American players were using it. For a while half of the Latin players would wait at one exit and the other half at the other. But they still weren't getting rides and in frustration went to their coach. He hadn't been aware of the situation, and in colorful language Freddy won't repeat, he made it clear he was upset with what had been going on. He also made sure the Latin players did not have to take any more cabs. They could pay their teammates for gas, but their teammates would be the ones taking them to the ballpark.

The next year things were better, but not on the field, not for Freddy. They started out okay, even well. In April Freddy was named the team's defensive player of the month for his steady play in right field, thirty-two putouts and three assists in eighteen games. Then a fight broke out during one game, and Freddy was hit in the face with a catcher's mask. He was out for a week with a concussion, and after that nothing was the same.

Sometimes he couldn't see the ball; other times he just tried too hard. It was his sixth year in professional baseball. It was a critical year, and he knew a decision would be made about his future. It came the following spring when the Astros released him. Freddy thought about going back to the Dominican Republic and playing there in the hopes of getting picked up by another Major League team. And he did that for a while, but he could stay only so long. In 2003 he had fallen in love with a Lexington girl, and in 2004 they had married. He had begun the long process toward obtaining U.S. citizenship and at that point could not be gone from the country for more than three months at a time.

It was a strange twist of fate. Freddy wasn't going to be a professional baseball player, but he had married the type of girl he had set his sights on around the time he started playing ball, one with blue eyes and blonde hair. His mother told him he declared that was the type of girl he was going to marry after a neighborhood girl, one with dark hair and dark eyes, told him she liked him. Freddy told her he had other plans. He was seven at the time.

Years later those other plans brought him back to Lexington. He thought about trying to play independent baseball. But a guy he knew who had done that ended up losing his house while trying to get back into affiliated baseball. And even the players he knew who made it back into affiliated baseball didn't stay long, or if they did, they didn't play much. He didn't want to do that, didn't want to risk so much for so little. So he stopped playing and started working. Now he helps with baseball camps, tournaments, and instruction at a local baseball academy.

His goal is to coach college baseball, but for that he will need a college degree, something he isn't quite ready to pursue. If his son, Freddy Jr., wants to play baseball, he won't stop him, but he won't be the one putting the bat in his hand. When his wife suggests he coach his son in T-ball, he tells her no; he'll let the coach do the coaching. "I just be the dad."

●

At the pregame meeting Andy Shea's dad takes the seat to the right of his son. William Shea is dressed like everyone else on staff in a Legends polo shirt, khaki shorts, and a baseball cap. The only thing distinguishing the owner from his employees is his age—he is about twice as old as most of them. The meeting takes place in the executive board room, a formal room separated from the general office with a view of the field. Before it gets started two employees gaze out on the field and talk about a different kind of sport—football.

Today is the big college in-state rivalry game between the University of Kentucky, in Lexington, and the University of Louisville, and the game is shown on a large screen above Applebee's Park. Kickoff was about an hour ago at Papa John's Cardinal Stadium in Louisville, and the game should be over by the time the Legends start playing. But it will still probably affect attendance. So will the fact that it is the Saturday of Labor Day weekend. But that doesn't mean the stands will be empty. At the start of the meeting a handout is passed around on which are listed all of the night's activities—contests, promotions, trophy presentations, and first pitches.

One by one the dozen or so employees—mostly male, mostly under forty—take turns explaining what they will be doing tonight: which birthday party they are working, what trophy presentations they are making, which large groups they have. Every once in a while someone asks for clarification: "Is it Estill County Exception Sports or Exceptional?" It's the latter, but on the sheet it is printed as both in different places. Someone else points out the group he is looking after is Central Kentucky Obstetrics, not Berry Campbell. Not even close. The others get a good laugh out of that before reporting on what they have going on—a marriage proposal, the parking situation, minimum bids for ten-year-anniversary jerseys.

When it's his turn, William reminds the staff that they are a few short tonight, that it is the last weekend, that it has been a great season, and to finish strong. His son, Andy, the front-office general manager, expounds a little more about how great the staff did handling a Hall of Fame presentation the night before. Then he thanks them. The whole thing is over in about fifteen minutes.

The season has taken a lot longer. And for the office staff it has been more intense than ever before thanks to all the non-Legends events they have held. It has gone well, but it has been unbelievably tiring and taxing, with only two or three weekends off the entire season. And they aren't finished yet. The Legends play their last game Monday, but there is still a country music concert coming up and a mixed martial arts competition. The performances won't end until the weather starts cooling in October. At that point Andy's weekends will be free, at least until his bar opens in December.

He visited his future bar earlier today with his father, who is in town from Pennsylvania for the weekend. The Legends are only one of his father's many ventures, and so he isn't here for most games. Andy plans to run his bar business the same way his father handles the Legends. He'll help on the business side of things, but the day-to-day management will be done by his business partner. There will be no phone line for him at the bar, not even an office.

Before he made it to the bar, Andy had lunch with his little brother, Christian, at Buffalo Wild Wings. They moved their weekly visits from Thursday to Saturday after his little brother started football and was having trouble making Thursday visits. Two Saturdays ago he took Christian and some of his friends to a game. He gave one of the kids a Legends T-shirt, and in exchange he received a plastic bracelet. He still wears the bracelet on his right wrist.

And he still talks about the special events they held this year. He may still be talking about them at the start of next season. That is because if someone went to a rock concert last Saturday, he says, they wouldn't necessarily come out this week for one of the Legends' last eight games, but they know Applebee's Park now, and hopefully next spring they will come to a ball game.

They may not see Jiovanni Mier. The shortstop is more than ready to go and already shipped his beloved Chevy Tahoe home to California. He has a plane ticket out of here for 7:00 a.m. Tuesday and after arriving in California at 10:35 in the morning plans to head straight to his favorite Mexican restaurant. He won't be traveling alone. During his girlfriend's last visit to Lexington he picked up a puppy, a male dachshund–shih tzu mix he calls Peanut. The furry purchase wasn't totally spontaneous. Jiovanni had wanted to get another dog ever since he lost his last dog, Pretty, a chow-shepherd mix. Pretty was fourteen and ran away two days after Jiovanni left his childhood home for spring training.

There have been other changes since Jiovanni left home. On August 30 his first nephew was born. He plans to visit the little guy in Arizona shortly after arriving home. The rest of the off-season he plans to spend with his brother, Jessie, the one who doesn't have a newborn and plays baseball for the AA Chattanooga Lookouts. Or at least Jessie played baseball until he fractured his thumb and had to have surgery on it a few weeks ago. He is currently in Arizona rehabbing.

Jiovanni had a healthier season and was happier with the second half than the first. He swung better, and in August his batting average was up to .304. But his slow start earlier in the season means his overall numbers weren't great—batting .235, with 2 home runs and 15 stolen bases in 131 games. One sports reporter went so far as to refer to his season as horrendous.

He wants to come back a lot stronger next season and plans to live with Jessie this summer and work on hitting, throwing, and just about everything else. The Astros want him to work hard as well, and after twelve days off they will be sending him to Florida for a month of instructional league, or extra practice.

He did it last year as well, and it is considered a good thing, a way to get to play more, to improve more.

But right now Jiovanni is ready for a break from baseball and the monotony of his life here in Lexington. The beautiful weather today, a humidity-free eighty degrees with a slight breeze, isn't helping him focus. It reminds him of the mild California weather he will soon be experiencing. The last three games are tough, a struggle between wanting to finish strong and wanting to get it over with. "It's kind of a teeter-totter, where you're going back and forth, like, got to do good, and, at the same time, don't care," he says.

It's a far cry from how he handled big games back in high school. Then he was known for puking on the field. Soccer championships, baseball playoffs, it didn't matter—there would be Jio throwing up, said his mother, Leticia. His brother did the same thing. Thankfully, Jio seems to have outgrown it in the Minors, she said. He could have gone on to play soccer or baseball, but the latter was always his first love. She credits the former with giving him fast feet for baseball. That and the dancing. "He loves to dance. Don't let him fool you on that. He loves salsa, cha-cha, merengue," said Leticia.

On the field before the game it is like the last days of school before summer vacation. Two players on the opposing team toss a baseball straight up in the air and jump to see who can grab it or knock it away first, kind of like a jump ball in basketball. There aren't too many fans tonight, but Legends president Alan Stein greets them just as energetically as always, squeezing shoulders, pumping hands, and calling out hellos as he walks along the main concourse. There will be fans lost to the college football rivalry game, but he isn't worried. He is a big University of Kentucky supporter and has season tickets to football, basketball, and baseball games, even though there isn't much chance of his making too many UK baseball games.

Before the Legends game he had the football game on in his office. When it ended with UK winning 23–16, the score was announced over the loudspeakers and shown on a big screen above the field. With the game over and the weather perfect, more people may start showing up.

The weather has been in the Legends' favor all season. Usually, they average about twenty-five to thirty weather-impacted games, but this year they had only seventeen, only one of which was an actual rainout. With the good weekend forecast, Alan thinks the seventeen will hold through the end of the season on Monday.

After that, while others are taking a little break, Alan will be gearing up again. In his job the hardest work happens when baseball isn't being played, a scenario he compares to a Broadway show, with the raising of money, the rehearsing, the writing, and the underwriting happening beforehand. "Once the season starts, it's like the curtain going up. You turn it over to the actors," he says.

At present the actors are members of youth teams being recognized during a pregame ceremony. The festivities involve the presentation of trophies to several local children's teams who are invited to be honored on the field before the game. A Legends staff member reads out the children's names, talks about their season, and compliments them on their snazzy jackets. Then he offers the crowd his own insights. "We love having little ones out here. Because who knows, you could be looking at a future Lexington Legend."

There is a little clapping, and then the real actors take the stage. Their performance this season has been less than stellar. The Legends lost their field manager midseason and are set to finish in the middle of the South Atlantic League's Southern Division.

Jiovanni's season mirrors the team's mediocre performance. He started off struggling, needing to make a lot of adjustments, says batting coach Stubby Clapp. But in the past month he has matured, adds Stubby, which has translated into better results offensively and defensively. Jiovanni, he says, has great and uncanny ability and has yet to reach his full potential.

Tonight's game starts out kind of like Jiovanni's season. In the top of the first inning an infield single bounds out of his glove, but Jiovanni is able to recover and throw a runner out at the plate. The fans seem to enjoy watching him, just like Stubby has enjoyed watching him this season. Of course, Stubby isn't the only one in the organization with eyes on Jiovanni. Those higher up are watching as well. "There's no doubt they know every move he makes," says Stubby.

Next season they will be rewarded for their attention. Jio will still be in Lexington at the start of the season, but his playing will have improved dramatically. Alan will also be back in his basement office at Applebee's Park. The park is like his middle son Scooter's second home. Scooter is twenty-one years old. His father's baseball dream existed long before he did. It started coming to fruition when Scooter was in grade school. By the time Scooter was in high school, it absorbed much of his father's time.

As a child Scooter dreamed of one day being his dad. Then he grew up and realized he had different interests. After six summers spent working at the ballpark, he got tired of it. He attends Butler University in Indianapolis, Indiana, and is looking to go into international relations. He doesn't see himself, or either of his two siblings, following their father into the business. Baseball is his dad's calling, not his. And he recognizes it is a calling. "People say he has the best job ever. I say, 'Come on, people, this is a guy who works seventy to eighty hours a week and is on the road flying across the country for about two days a week,'" said Scooter. "His passion—if he didn't have it, I don't know how long he'd be in the job."

Kathy dreams of retirement and a time when her husband has time to read, relax, and play golf. But she knows that is her dream. Alan's is here. Over the years Alan has had multiple opportunities to move to the Major Leagues, said his friend Billy Forbess. "He chooses not to because this is his home, where his family and friends are, and he loves Minor League Baseball," said Billy.

His sister, Teri Stein Harper, has talked to Alan about slowing down, told him he's not going to do them any good if he's dead at sixty, but he just looks at her like she's crazy, she said. With the Legends, Alan has combined his love of baseball with his love of Lexington. His son Scooter probably sums it up best: "The Legends are his life."

Lexington Legends president Alan
Stein and his wife, Kathy, cheer on
the team. By James Calvert.

2. (*Above*) Shortstop Jiovanni Mier leaving the dugout at Applebee's Park. By James Calvert.

3. (*Opposite top*) Shortstop Jiovanni Mier and second baseman Jose Altuve in the stands of Applebee's Park. By James Calvert.

4. (*Opposite bottom*) Applebee's Park head groundskeeper Chris Pearl and his nine-year-old son, Zachary, a.k.a. "Mini Pearl." By James Calvert.

5. (*Opposite top*) Legends second baseman Jose Altuve in the two-bedroom condo he shares with eight other Latin players. By James Calvert.

7 (*Above*) Jiovanni Mier in the condo he shares with three other players. By James Calvert.

6. (*Opposite bottom*) Legends shortstop Jiovanni Mier and his girlfriend, Kristen Lawson, in his bedroom. By James Calvert.

8. (*Top*) Legends shortstop Jiovanni Mier and his girlfriend, Kristen Lawson, in his condo. Curtains in the background mark off a teammate's room. By James Calvert.

9. Jiovanni Mier and Kristen Lawson wait to pick up the other players and take them to the park. By James Calvert.

Part 2
Louisville Bats:
A Lesson in Discontent

5. Great Expectations

If the Louisville Bats were my introduction to the Minors, Kevin Barker was my guide to disillusionment. When I met him at the start of the 2009 season, Kevin was in his midthirties, with not much of a future, no family of his own, and no real home. He made it clear he didn't want to spend another season in the Minors, yet that is where he was, playing first base for the Bats, the AAA affiliate of the Cincinnati Reds. He didn't know his address. He didn't need to. His mail was sent to the ballpark, and he didn't entertain many visitors. He knew how to get to his apartment, he knew how to get to Louisville Slugger Field, and he knew the reason I wanted to write about him was not because he was on his way up, but because he was on his way out.

I was going to spend the season following several players for a newspaper series on life in the Minors. Kevin originally agreed to be one of the players I profiled. He gave me his phone number, but never returned my calls. We would arrange to meet, and then he would stand me up. I got what I needed through his parents and by standing outside the clubhouse waiting for Kevin to exit. At the end of the season the Cincinnati Reds recalled him. Kevin was back in the Majors. His mother told me the family's prayers had been answered.

Kevin didn't get picked up for the 2010 season. He is playing in Mexico. Baseball, especially in the Minors, is often a game of disappointment. But on opening day, as long as the sun is shining, the season seems filled with possibility.

That is definitely the case in Louisville at the start of the 2010 season. For the past two years the Bats have won more games than any other team in the International League. They finished last season with the best record in the league (84-58) and their second consecutive West Division title. Their roster includes Aroldis Chapman, a Cuban defector many are calling the sport's top import, and eight of the Reds' top prospects as rated by *Baseball America*.

Pitcher Matt Maloney is one of the eight top prospects. Reds manager Dusty Baker called Matt's big league debut against the Chicago Cubs last season, during which he faced quite a bit of adversity, "outstanding." Matt allowed leadoff doubles in three of his first four innings, hit the second batter he faced with a pitch, and got out of a bases-loaded jam in the second inning with back-to-back strikeouts. He received a standing ovation from a packed Great American Ball Park when Baker replaced him in the seventh inning. Afterward Baker talked of Matt's poise and savvy. Matt called the whole experience "awesome." He's back with the Bats now, but no one expects him to stay long.

Same goes for Chris Burke, a utility player whose home run launched the Houston Astros into the National League Championship Series in 2005. Chris played thirty-two games for the San Diego Padres last season before asking for his release. He finished the season in AAA with the Gwinnett Braves in Lawrenceville, Georgia, for the Atlanta Braves, but expects to be back in the Majors with the Reds before long. Still, this is baseball, and the season is long and unpredictable. Before it is over both Matt and Chris will be in situations few would have imagined opening day. So will the team.

But that comes later. Right now it's a little before six, more than an hour before game time on Louisville Slugger Field's eleventh annual opening night. Since much of the Louisville Bats' front-office staff have been around almost as long as the stadium, team president Gary Ulmer isn't too worried about logistics. Still, he has exchanged his black wing tips for a pair of brown Rockport shoes he uses to make his rounds. He learned early on to keep spare clothing at the ballpark. Upstairs in his office he has two pairs of shoes stashed under his desk, a suit hanging behind his door, and a couple of pairs of khaki pants at the ready.

He also learned early on how many laps around the stadium equals a mile—three—information more valuable now that he is fifty-three and the pizza and chips served in the press room are starting to take a toll. Not that you would know it by looking at him, as he is tall and slim and always takes the stairs.

As team president Gary is probably the only person on staff who doesn't have a place he has to be, or a job he has to do tonight. So he walks the stadium, noting a cigarette butt pushed into a corner (there is a no-smoking policy, so it shouldn't be there), picking up stray balls ("That's ten dollars right there," he says, pocketing two balls), and greeting workers who have returned for another season.

There is the television meteorologist dressed in shorts for the balmy seventy-plus-degree night, the concession-stand man who just got promoted and is wearing a tie and dress shirt that, Gary observes, "he'll sweat through in no time," and an elderly usher now busy wiping down seats. When it gets closer to game time, Gary heads outside the west gate entrance to keep an eye on the line, greet the team's owners, and otherwise make sure things are running smoothly at one of the busier entrances.

He greets season-ticket holders like old friends, welcoming them back for another year, remarking on the wonderful weather, and asking after their health. The only thing he doesn't mention is their names. He never learned them, and after ten years he doesn't feel right asking. It's something he wishes he had done differently. But then, he didn't know they would be here this long—or that he would.

Before Slugger Field was built, and Gary was researching other ballparks, he discovered that some experience a downward spiral after six or seven years. Attendance starts to dwindle, the park raises prices, attendance dwindles further, and things just get worse and worse. It wasn't a picture Gary had any intention of being around to see, so he figured he would stay a half-dozen years or so before moving on to something else. Ten years later business is good, the ballpark is beautiful, and he is still here. Upstairs in his office is a photo of the site before its November 1998 groundbreaking. "Scrap was piled up to the edge of the interstates. That was what you looked at when you came into Louisville," he says.

The site was an "environmental cesspool" covered with dirt and garbage. There was also a dilapidated train depot Gary thought would have to be torn down. The architects saw it differently: they thought integrating the historical depot into the project would make a perfect entryway to the ballpark. They were right. "I saw it after a while, but I didn't see it then," Gary admits.

What he did see was that if the team didn't get a new stadium, it was pretty much doomed. Since his father, Dan Ulmer, had helped bring professional baseball back to Louisville in 1982, after an almost decadelong absence, the game had changed. In the early 1980s Louisville helped lead a sort of Minor League renaissance. Great crowds came to see what it was all about. During the 1983 regular season Louisville was the first Minor League team to draw more than one million people.[1]

But as time went on the thrill began to wear off, and fans started to notice that the facility where the team played was old and lacking in modern amenities, he says. At the same time, he says, business groups around the country were taking over teams and building new stadiums in downtown areas. Suddenly, Louisville, with its 1950s-era Cardinal Stadium with an artificial-turf field, located at the state fairgrounds south of downtown, wasn't looking so good. "So we went from best to nowhere near best ten years later," Gary says.

His father had helped make the team one of the finest in AAA. Gary wanted to be the one to bring them back to the top. It was the early 1990s, and he hadn't been in baseball since a brief stint in the lower levels of the front-office staff when he was young, single, and the son of the man in charge.

Around the time of the Major League player strike of 1981, Gary's father, Dan, then president of Citizens Fidelity Bank, cochaired a committee that raised more than four million dollars to revamp a football stadium and wooed the St. Louis Cardinals' AAA Redbirds from Springfield, Illinois.[2] There wasn't a lot of staff, so Gary got on board in sales. He came back almost a decade later as president, after having spent the intervening years in the banking business. His initial job, he says, was to come up with a long-term strategy for the team's survival, and his focus became a new downtown stadium. He knows if his family hadn't helped to bring professional baseball back and build a downtown stadium, someone else probably would have. It's a strange family heritage, banks and ballparks.

Thanks to his banking background, Gary still starts his work-day around seven-thirty or eight in the morning, even though he works in a sport that doesn't really get going until afternoon and often continues into the evening. But then, as president, Gary isn't concerned with the outcome of the games as much as he is with health insurance, liability insurance, cost containment, and personnel matters. When people ask if he travels with the team, he tells them the team manager doesn't need him. But if the copy machine breaks down in the office, he's needed. "So it's business first for me and baseball second," he says.

And by opening day the business part of baseball is pretty much done—advertising, season tickets; the bulk are either sold or not. Of course, he knows fans still care about what happens on the field, and he expects them to be pleased this year. Spectators will no doubt be clamoring to see Aroldis Chapman's fastball, which has been clocked at one hundred miles per hour. They will probably also be excited to see hometown favorite Chris Burke and a number of highly touted prospects. With repeat league manager of the year Rick Sweet once again at the helm, the team is in good hands, and Gary knows it. He is looking forward to a winning season.

Right now, though, he is worried not about the Bats living up to their reputation, but about remembering the names of the people throwing out the ceremonial first pitches, a task made more difficult because he has left his cheat sheet in his office.

He gets around it by offering tips to the handful of men lining up on the side of the field to throw. "For starters, no one ever boos if it's high, only when they bounce three times," he says. The men—bankers, radiomen, and others from companies that sponsor or otherwise support the Bats—listen attentively as Gary advises them to aim high to compensate for the mound. When they take to the mound he rates their throws. A tall guy in penny loafers garners a nine out of ten, a banker a "wow."

Up in the stands a few minutes later, loaded down with baseballs, Gary suffers a little ribbing from his father and other team owners who ask if he is after autographs. Dressed in khakis and loafers, they blend in with the rest of the business crowd catching the game at the end of the workday. There is no owner's suite—they gave that up after learning they could rent it for one thousand dollars a night, says Gary. Instead, they sit in a small area at the top of the stands behind home plate. Mostly white-haired and balding, they will have to yield power to another generation before too long. Gary has three children of his own, but doesn't expect them to follow in their father's or grandfather's footsteps. One of his sons plays baseball at the same Catholic high school Gary attended, and where he now serves on the board, but that is just how things are in Louisville.

A river city of about 722,000, Louisville is neither completely southern nor midwestern; people seem to either never leave here or return when they are ready to settle down. In a way Chris Burke is happy to be home. What better place to try to get back into the Majors than on a AAA team surrounded by family and friends. As he takes the plate in the bottom of the first inning a loud cheer erupts, and Gary steps forward to get a better look. He knows Chris and his family, even serves with his brother on a local board. Chris's parents and his brother, Paul, are here tonight. Paul played in the Minors but blew out his shoulder before making it further than Class-A. He thinks it's pretty neat that his kid brother is the hometown hero, but like everyone else he is counting on Chris being back in the Majors before long.

Although Matt Maloney's performance with the Reds last year wasn't stellar—he finished with a 4.87 earned run average in seven games—a strong spring-training showing this season kept the lefty on the Major League roster up until the day before the team left Arizona and headed east. Now the 2005 Philadelphia Phillies' third-round draft pick is in Louisville watching the game until it is his night to pitch. His wife, Kalee, sits in the stands by herself.

Until opening night it didn't really hit her how strange it would be to be back in Louisville without the players' wives and girlfriends she spent so much time with last year. So many of them are gone: one woman and her two girls are down in AA, while another woman has followed her husband to the Majors. Only Kalee is back in the stands, trying to get to know a new set of women she may have little in common with. Many are obsessed with the game, she explains, checking their phones constantly to see how things stand in the Majors and when their husbands might move up.

Kalee wants Matt to be in the bigs, but she also wants to enjoy what they have now—their two dogs, their friends, and everything that constitutes life outside the ballpark. Finding other women like herself sitting in the family section of the stands behind home plate is hard, which is why when she finds them, she tries to hold on to them. But that isn't something she can control. Early in tonight's game she introduced herself to a blonde woman sitting two seats down. Now, a few innings later, she mistakenly calls the woman Jessica, only to learn that's not her name. They both laugh, an instant understanding of how hard it is to keep track of things when you, and everyone around you, are always in motion.

Matt finished last season in Cincinnati, but Kalee finished it in Louisville. She returned their rented furniture a month before their October lease was up, so after the Reds' season ended and Matt was back in Louisville, they slept on an air mattress and watched their television propped on a plastic storage bin. Looking back, Kalee laughs, "I don't know why I thought that would be comfortable for a month." Not just any month, but the month before their wedding. In the end the young couple—Matt is twenty-six, Kalee twenty-four—drove back to their hometown of Sandusky, Ohio, a few days early so they could sleep in a real bed and get things ready for their November wedding.

Two days after saying their "I dos," they were on the road again. This time they were headed to Austin, Texas, a place neither of them had ever been. A honeymoon for the Maloneys was staying in one place for more than a month, says Kalee, and in that sense Austin counted. They stayed in a vacation rental they shared with Matt's best man, Reds pitcher Daniel Ray Herrera. They ended up in Austin because they wanted to spend the off-season somewhere warm and because it came recommended by a number of other ballplayers they know. The rooming arrangement was a way to save money so they could rest, instead of getting part-time jobs or Matt playing winter ball in Latin America.

They continued the arrangement in Arizona for spring training. After paying for much of their wedding, says Kalee, they were counting every penny and even downsized to a single vehicle. Matt made about eight thousand dollars a month last year when he was in AAA, Kalee estimates, but that is only for the months he was playing baseball. His signing bonus in 2005 was four hundred thousand dollars.

The apartment complex where they live in Louisville is situated on a hill above the river among a cluster of similar complexes. It's the same place Matt and Kalee stayed last season and the place Kalee decided to reserve at the last minute when they still didn't know where Matt would be playing.

If Matt made the Reds' opening-day roster, they figured they could crash with Daniel until finding a place of their own. But if he was back down in Louisville, they knew they would need a place right away. So with a week left in spring training Kalee reserved a two-bedroom, two-bath apartment in Louisville. Then she booked a plane ticket to Cincinnati.

It makes sense, in a way only life in the Minors makes sense. Matt would be traveling with his teammates, either by plane or by bus. He didn't want Kalee to make the thirty-hour drive from Arizona on her own, so they paid a thousand dollars to ship their truck to Cincinnati and several hundred more to get Kalee and their two dogs to Cincinnati. They planned to meet up there. If Matt ended up in Louisville, they would drive the two hours there together.

Only Kalee and the dogs arrived on Saturday; the truck and Matt didn't come until Sunday. From the airport Kalee called the wife of a player who lived in town and arranged to crash at her house. The next day, after the truck and Matt arrived, they drove to Louisville, where they spent the night in a hotel eating bar food. It was Easter, and the office of their apartment complex wasn't open.

When they got into their apartment the next day, they stayed only long enough to look around before getting back on the road to retrieve some of their belongings. All during last season and the off-season Matt insisted he never felt like he was home, so Kalee decided the best way to remedy this would be to bring their stuff with them this time. Since the season started they have been on the road almost nonstop traveling to games and retrieving their various belongings from storage in Ohio. They arrived back in Louisville at one in the morning before the team's home opener tonight. Just recounting the experience takes Kalee well into the seventh inning of a game that the Bats end up losing 0–3.

•

Two days after opening night they are still unpacking. Matt is hunched over a sports bag in their guest room, sorting through some of his stuff before he has to head to the field for tonight's game. He holds up a Boston Red Sox baseball hat and a Cleveland Indians one as well. "Can't really wear these hats right now, can I?" he says, tossing them aside.

Tall and lanky, he is a bit of a comedian. A season or two ago he tried to superglue a coach's pen to a board in the dugout. When I first met him at the start of the 2009 season he was a goofy prospect who deflected attention by putting his teammates in the hot seat. On the road when I asked to follow them to lunch, fellow prospect Drew Stubbs seemed uncomfortable and evasive, but Matt just went along with it. While his teammates worried about overeating before the game, Matt didn't think twice about ordering the dinner entrée, and eating it all. Kevin Barker walked by the restaurant and Matt pounded on the window, trying to get him to join them. When Matt was called up, quite a few of his teammates got watery eyes, said Bats pitching coach Ted Power. Even the clubhouse manager called Matt a good guy.

Now he rushes through the process of sorting through his

stuff as Kalee follows behind, rescuing his barely used baseball caps and sports shoes from the garbage pile and depositing them in a giveaway pile. A few fan letters sit on the dining room table, lost in the confusion of the end of last season and only recently rediscovered. Matt holds one up, a letter written in large block letters with creative grammar and spelling. Kalee thinks it might be from a kid and wants Matt to answer it. Matt thinks it is probably from an old man who added the spelling errors and bad grammar so it would look like it was from a child. There is no way to know who is right, but if there is no card for Matt to sign, and no stamped self-addressed envelope to send it back in, he doesn't bother trying to figure it out. None of the ballplayers do, he says. The fans know the rules, and so do the players. From the mail pile, he signs a homemade Matt Maloney baseball card.

His fingers are long and bear two distinguishing marks, both on his left hand: his wife's initials on his ring finger, in place of a wedding band, and a hardened scab on the tip of another finger. His life story is told on a tattoo on the inside of his left forearm. It is a tree at the bottom of which is his date of birth, 01/16/84. The branches contain his Major League debut, 06/06/09, and wedding day, 11/14/09. There is room for children later. Right now he is focused on the second date, the date he made it to the Majors, allowing two runs on six hits while striking out four in the Reds' eleventh-inning 4–3 victory over the Cubs.

He played a few more games, returned to the Bats, and was promoted again for the end of the season, continuing to pitch despite the blister on his pitching hand, which was causing him increasing pain and numbness. He figured he was earning his spot on the roster. And the Reds might have seen it that way as well, only, in the end, they didn't.

When Matt learned he would be back in AAA for a third

season, he made it clear he wasn't pleased. But the Reds' farm system is stacked with young talent this year, including Aroldis Chapman, a left-handed pitcher for whom they paid $30.25 million. "I think they know he [Matt] doesn't want to be buried in AAA," says Kalee. He feels he should be playing in the Majors, and he is determined that that is where he will be this season. To get there he does the best he can at this level. Before opening night he made two starts and won them both. In his last start he mixed different speeds and pitches in allowing only two runs.

Soon he will need to leave for tonight's game. It's a little before one o'clock, and the game isn't until seven, but there are practice, weights, and a lot of other work to be done at the ballpark. In the hall across the way a few of his teammates are starting to move about. One comes over to borrow a cup of ice; another walks his dog out back. More than a half-dozen players live in the complex this season, many of them following the Maloneys' advice. Matt plans to ride to the field with a teammate and asks Kalee if she needs him to leave her a ticket. She does. He kisses her good-bye. She tells him to have a good day at the field. Then she shouts across the way, asking the guys to leave her a key so she can retrieve her dishes from their dishwasher. The Maloneys' dishwasher has flooded.

6. Pitch Perfect

Special press conferences are held just for Aroldis Chapman. Individual interviews are impossible. The Reds are keeping a close watch on their $30.25 million investment, a rookie pitcher who has been clocked at one hundred miles per hour.

But Aroldis isn't the only reason sports analysts are predicting that the Bats' strength will be in their starting pitching this season. The rotation includes Sam LeCure, who tied for fourth in the league in strikeouts last year (125); Travis Wood, who is rated the Reds' seventh-best prospect by *Baseball America*; and Matt Maloney, the Bats' most consistent starter last year.

Then there is Charles Larry "Justin" Lehr, the International League's most valuable pitcher. Justin spent the second half of last season in the Majors and is coming off what he believes was one of his best spring-training camps. In previous seasons Justin pitched remarkably well for the Bats and proved he could pitch in the big leagues when he was up with the Reds, said Bats pitching coach Ted Power. All of which is reason to believe Justin might be in for one of the better performances of his professional career.

Most likely it will be overshadowed by Aroldis. But that doesn't bother Justin—he is used to being in the background, being underestimated. When he was a kid his family didn't take his dreams of playing professionally seriously, for most of his college career he was a catcher, not a pitcher, and he was drafted his senior instead of his junior year. But Justin always knew he wanted to play professional baseball, and those were not the only challenges he overcame.

His family thought his baseball dreams would pass. He'd get interested in girls, his father warned, but Justin was surrounded by them at home. He grew up in Southern California with his mother, a homemaker, and three sisters. He wasn't distracted by girls. School didn't pose much of a diversion, either. He hadn't thought about college until he started getting letters from colleges his junior year in high school. He hadn't even been taking many college preparatory classes. His SAT scores weren't great. Neither were his grades, but he got into the University of California at Santa Barbara on an athletic scholarship.

He chose UCSB because it wasn't far from home and because he would be able to play catcher on the baseball team. He wanted to play every day, and he wanted to play professionally. Catching, he thought, would provide him with the best chance of doing both. But coaches seemed to think Justin should pitch, something he did occasionally in high school, and eventually he agreed. He transferred to the University of Southern California after his junior year and became a pitcher. He has pitched ever since, either as a starter or coming out of the bullpen as a reliever.

He was drafted by the Oakland Athletics in the eighth round in 1999. As a junior he might have gotten a $70,000 to $80,000 signing bonus in the same round that year. As a senior he had little leverage, though, except to go to independent ball, and no one, he says, was going to do that. So he signed for $20,000. Although he spent four years in college, he did not have enough credits to graduate, and now, all these years later, he is twenty credits shy of a sociology degree. His wife, Guia, finished school, but starting a career for her has been nearly impossible.

Justin wasn't born with as much talent as Aroldis, so he and Guia have had to make sacrifices to get him where he is, including her career. The first five years of the marriage she followed Justin from city to city and team to team as he climbed the Minor League ladder. She worked jobs that fitted her mobile lifestyle: sales, tutoring, and as a substitute teacher.

In the off-season Justin joined her in the classroom. It was a strange choice for a guy who was never really into school, but he liked the pay. When he and his wife were teaching, the two of them could bring in $3,500 to $4,000 a month, and Justin was making about $10,000 for an entire year in AAA.

Another off-season he spent in Puerto Rico playing winter ball. His wife, then pregnant with their first child, went with him. In late 2003 they bought a house in Arizona, and soon after their son, Reed, was born. Justin started the 2004 season in AAA in Sacramento, California, again, making about $2,500 a month. Guia was no longer working, and with two households to support, Justin's paycheck wasn't enough. He had to ask his father for a $2,500 loan. In the five years he had been playing it was the first time he had to ask his father for money.

He got called up a few days later and immediately returned the money. The promotion was significant both professionally and financially. Now on the club's forty-man roster, Justin's salary climbed to $10,000 or $12,000 a month. He was originally called up because another player was on bereavement leave, but ended up staying most of the season. "It's funny how the game works like that," he says.

After his 2004 stint in the Majors he was traded to the Milwaukee Brewers. In 2005 he just barely missed making the big league team and left spring training believing that he'd be back in the Majors as soon as the Brewers called up a relief pitcher in about two weeks. So he went down to AAA, he says, "and got killed." In his third game of the season for the Nashville Sounds he gave up something like eight runs without recording an out, and after four games his ERA had ballooned to around 67. He wasn't called up after the two weeks had passed. In the end, he managed to lower his ERA to a respectable 3.99 and was promoted in late July.

Five years later he is sitting in the Bats' dugout in Louisville on a Tuesday afternoon in early May. Unfortunately, the start of this season is proving to be a bit of a repeat of the start of his 2005 season. Not unlike in 2005 he had a great chance to make the Major League team and not only didn't make it but began his regular season badly. This year that means three losses and no wins and a 6.64 ERA in April. Still, the season is long, and there is no reason to think he won't make the same kind of turnaround he did in 2005.

In the meantime, he is looking forward to having his son, Reed, sit in the dugout with him during games. He probably couldn't do that in the bigs, but the rules are more relaxed in AAA. Justin hopes he can work something out when his wife, his son, and his daughter, three-year-old Avery, come up to visit later this season from Arizona. Last year they were supposed to stay with him for two months, but six days into their stay he got traded to the Reds. So they went home, and he came to Louisville. This year he has gone ahead and rented an apartment in Louisville his family will be able to share with him when they come. It's a difficult, unpredictable life, and at thirty-two Justin knows it could end any day. "You could have one good year, one bad, and then done," he says. "That's just the reality."

Many of his former teammates are out of baseball. Justin isn't ready to leave yet. He has given up too much, and he started the season with too much promise to simply walk away. He is the kind of guy you can't help but root for; he wasn't born with a ton of talent, money, or connections, just a dream and determination to do what it takes to get what he wants. He has the dogged determination to be back in the bigs, and it just seems like a matter of time before he gets there.

Matt Maloney has also made sacrifices to get where he is, like missing his wife Kalee's college graduation. But he has always had one man in his corner, his father, Joe Maloney. "He basically did everything he could to help me be the best I could possibly be," said Matt.

A natural athlete, Matt never doubted he would play professionally, just wavered on the sport; in fall it was football, in winter basketball, in spring baseball. It was only when he was twelve and his father suggested he move up to the high school baseball team that he knew his sport would probably be baseball. In Matt's freshmen year in high school his father turned the backyard into a batting cage. He built another batting cage in the basement.

At Matt's big league debut last season Joe barely said a word, sitting silently with his wife, Kim, his hands clenched at his sides. When I asked to talk to him, he was hesitant. "Baseball is really superstitious," he said. "Usually we never talk to anyone during the game."

Joe's mother, Kathy Maloney, had warned me how serious her son took her grandson's playing. She sat in another section that day and was as loud as her son and daughter-in-law were quiet. Matt is her eldest grandson and one of her favorite topics. She talks about his childhood, when they called him "Little King Tut," a nickname she doesn't fully explain. She regularly calls the Bats' media relations director, asking for pictures and tickets and anything else that has to do with Matt's career. She told me she wanted to make puzzles out of a baseball picture of Matt to give to the other grandchildren.

Matt isn't as outspoken as his grandmother or as silent as his father, but somewhere in between, rather like his grandfather Jean Maloney. A retired engineer for Ford Motor Company, Jean is straightforward. "Truthfully, if it wasn't for [Matt], I thought baseball one of the most boring things I'd ever seen," he said.

Of course, now he follows it closely, especially the pitchers. His son, he said, has a lot of money invested in Matt. Joe is a factory man, Kim a receptionist. Their other son is a firefighter. They live in the small town of Sandusky, Ohio, where there were only about 130 people in Matt's graduating class. A few of Matt's former classmates were at his Major League debut, amazed that someone from Sandusky had made it to the Majors and still talked to them. "That's probably one of the neatest things, is how he keeps in touch with all of his friends back home, with everyone from back home," said Mike Eirons, a Cleveland insurance salesman who went to high school with Matt and was at his debut. That is, except the night before his debut, when Matt turned off his cell phone because he got so many texts and calls. It was while playing in the bigs last season that he aggravated a blister on the left middle finger of his pitching hand. For a few days this May the blister made it too painful for him to pitch.

But he is pitching again and throwing the ball well, with a 2.36 ERA the four games he pitched in May. By the second week of June he believes he is pitching at a Major League level—but there isn't a spot for him with the Reds. The Reds are stacked with starting pitchers, and they are playing well enough to make it to postseason play for the first time in years. In the meantime, the promising Bats are faltering. In late April and early May the Bats lost nine straight games. They are doing better now, but still not looking anything like the team that made it to the International League playoffs last year.

Matt has played with the team since 2007, and Louisville, just a five-hour drive from their family in Ohio, is starting to feel a little like home. He isn't the "veteran old guy" yet, but he is, in a way, a veteran. He's been around the league long enough to know a lot of the players on the other teams, to know what to expect from them on the field, and to know that it now falls on him to pass this knowledge on to his teammates playing in AAA for the first time.

Last year the old-guy role was played by thirty-four-year-old Kevin Barker, a first baseman who had been in the Majors a few times but in the Minors much longer. The loudmouth of the team, Kevin shared his opinions with everyone but otherwise kept to himself, kept hitting, and kept ending up back with the Bats. That is, until this year, when he was cut during spring training. Now he's in Mexico, playing well, like he has every-where he's played, says Matt. Matt has talked to him several times this season, usually during road trips when his roommate, reliever Jon Adkins, chats with Kevin via Internet video calls. "He looks skinny, looks like he's lost some weight," Matt says.

"I don't know how well he's eating down there in Mexico, but I know he's playing."

The hope is that if he keeps doing that, he can get himself a job back in the United States, says Matt. As he talks, the Steve Miller Band's tune "Fly Like an Eagle" comes out of speakers, drowning out the continuous crack of a bat hitting a ball during batting practice. Other former Bats are up in the Majors now. Last year Drew Stubbs played with Matt in Louisville but was called up to Cincinnati and is now the Reds' starting center fielder. Matt follows him from a distance while trying to stay focused on his own pitching. But what happens in Cincinnati directly affects Louisville. Matt's next scheduled start was pushed back a day because the Reds sent pitcher Homer Bailey down for a rehabilitation start in AAA.

The bus leaves tomorrow at 5:00 a.m. to take them to the airport for their next series in Syracuse. Last year the Bats traveled by chartered planes thanks to some special deal and could arrive at the airport close to takeoff, saving them several precious hours of sleep. But this year they are flying commercial, going through security and waiting in the airport like everyone else. It's particularly hard when a morning flight follows a night game. "Just another thing to let you know where you are," Matt says.

●

While most of the Bats are not well known, there is one exception as the 2010 season opens. By all the attention he is getting, it is hard to remember Aroldis Chapman is not in the big leagues, has never been in the big leagues, never even played professional baseball in the United States until this season. The left hander started the season with the Bats, and Tomas Vera has barely left his side since. Tomas translates for the twenty-two-year-old Cuban defector during press conferences, helps him find his way around, and generally takes on the role of big brother and friend. It isn't his job, but neither is about 85 percent of what he does on any given day.

Tomas is a trainer, and his job is the prevention of athletic injuries, a career for which he spent many years studying and secured multiple degrees. In the bigs he would spend all his time using those degrees, but in the Minors he also serves as travel secretary, pocket-money distributor, and a host of other unrelated duties. The front office arranges the road trips, but Tomas makes sure everything goes according to plan. "And beside that I'm the older brother, the psychologist for all these boys when they have marriage problem, girlfriend problem, when they have frustration on the field," he says. "And now, you can add to that, that I'm an Aroldis Chapman translator/right hand."

It isn't the path he envisioned. Back home in his native Venezuela he studied to be a physical education teacher. A big guy, with even bigger hands—his nickname is Manos, or "Hands"— Tomas has devoted much of his life to the same dream as the players: getting to the big leagues. At forty-two he is used to the constant travel, the long days, the frequent moves up the ladder. He administers treatments and therapies in the training room and educates players about the proper way to eat, warm up, and rest. He talks with Bats manager Rick Sweet daily about specific injuries and recommends when a player might need a rest day. For position players he mostly sees hand and knee injuries, for throwers shoulder and elbow problems.

He first started working with athletes while still in school in Venezuela and quickly decided he wanted to spend his life as a trainer. While working for a baseball team in Venezuela, he was invited by a Major League team to spring training in the United States. To become the kind of certified athletic trainer he wanted to be here, he needed to complete some course work and take a certification test. He failed the test five times, largely because he could not comprehend the English, and then he went back to school to take English-comprehension classes. He passed one part of the three-part test on the sixth try, another on the seventh, and the last on the ninth. Each time he took the test he had to pay several hundred dollars and wait several months before retaking it. In 2000 he finally passed everything and started climbing the same ladder the players do. In 2006 the Reds acquired his contract, and two years later he was assigned to the Bats.

He is closer to the big leagues, but not close enough. His days are long, and he is tired. He barely sees his wife, daughter, and son during the season. They all live in the United States. The family has a home in Sarasota, Florida. His son now plays Class-A ball for the Chicago White Sox. The schedule has taken its toll. For eight years Tomas didn't even have time to return to Venezuela and only finally did so last off-season.

For Tomas there is no time for anything but baseball during the season. He arrives at the field around noon and seldom leaves before midnight. Before the game he administers massages, ices and wraps injuries, and otherwise tends to the players' tired bodies. During the game he watches for injuries, signs of pain, and poor mechanics that can lead to injuries. After the game he writes a report of everything that happened. Then he goes home, oftentimes only to be called by the manager a half hour later to be told that they need a player in the big leagues the next day. So instead of going to sleep, he gets on the phone and the computer to arrange a plane ticket, transportation to and from the airport, and other details, including updating others in the organization about the plans. Then he goes to bed, only to be awoken at 6:00 a.m. by the player whose flight he just arranged, telling him he missed his flight. "Or maybe you got a 3:30 in the morning phone call with a guy saying, 'I missing my wife, I missing my family. I gonna walk into manager's office. I'm going to ask him for my release. I want to go home,'" he says. Then Tomas finds out where the guy is, usually at a bar, and goes there. He always manages to talk the player out of quitting. It isn't hard; he just asks them what their plans are, what they are going to do for work. And when they answer, and that answer is always "I don't know," Tomas has no trouble convincing them to keep playing until they figure it out.

His big-brother role extends even further with fellow Latinos. When they first arrive in the United States, he says, they don't have a concept of credit because they have always done everything in cash. That is the first thing they have to learn, about credit cards and credit reports. The second, he says, is respecting physical space, like wearing headphones when they want to listen to music because the guy next to them might not want to hear it. Food, of course, is a big issue, as adapting to the high-calorie fast food that fuels road trips can be an adjustment. And then there are mannerisms like saying "I'm sorry" and "Excuse me." "Americans like to hear that," says Tomas. Latin players aren't used to saying it, he says, because when you screw up in their countries, you don't say anything; you just move on. His newest charge, Aroldis Chapman, has had to learn even more. "When you're twenty-two and you have thirty million dollars in the bank, and you are free for the first time in your life, it's kind of difficult," says Tomas. "In a country like this you can go and buy whatever you want—everything you dream."

There are many things that aren't available in Cuba, says Tomas. Aroldis got a taste of what he was missing when he traveled around the world with the Cuban national team. His entire town saw an iPhone only when Aroldis brought one home following a trip to Japan with the national team. Internet access is so restricted and limited in Cuba, adds Tomas, that Aroldis's family back in Cuba cannot even type in reds.com to check his statistics. They are able to talk to him on cell phones, and he has been able to send some money home. But Aroldis has yet to meet his one-year-old daughter, born after he defected, and has no idea when he might see her.

In Louisville Aroldis is lost without his GPS, says Tomas. On the field he has also struggled, but Tomas chalks it up to inexperience. Aroldis never played college baseball, never played Minor League Baseball before this year, and took the sport up only at the age of fourteen. Before that he was a boxer, like his father. Aroldis can't be compared to American players who picked up their first baseball at three and have been playing some sort of organized form of the sport ever since. Besides, Tomas says, Aroldis makes up in talent what he lacks in experience. "In twenty-one years I haven't seen somebody with the quality, his quality, his talent, such immense talent. Hopefully, he can put it altogether," says Tomas.

Maybe he can, another night. At first Aroldis, tonight's starting pitcher, looks sharp, his fastball sizzling, usually clocking at around one hundred miles per hour. But Pawtucket's leadoff hitter singles, and by the time the inning ends Aroldis has given up two runs.

Charles Graham, a longtime usher in section 110 at Slugger Field, points out that Aroldis has been here longer than anyone thought he would. But after the first day he saw Aroldis pitch, Charles says he knew the Cuban would be here a while, because "he's a thrower, not a pitcher." His May starts showed promise but lack consistency. In two of the starts he gave up fourteen earned runs, but in the other three he allowed only one earned run.

Tonight against the Pawtucket Red Sox of Pawtucket, Rhode Island, Aroldis lasts only two innings. He gives up six hits and six walks and allows seven runs. He's wild. One pitch bounces in front of the plate; another almost hits the batter. A fan calls out, "What's this guy doing?" The catcher goes out to the mound to talk to Aroldis, then the pitching coach. The powwow takes place several times until Aroldis is finally taken out. It is a performance that holds so much expectation one moment, so much disappointment the next. But Tomas says the Cuban takes it in stride. "Aroldis Chapman doesn't frustrate," says Tomas. "He doesn't feel that; he doesn't feel any pressure. He know there are things he can control and things he cannot control." What Tomas doesn't know is that one of the things Aroldis will soon control is Tomas's future.

7. The Faithful

Pitcher Matt Maloney was golfing in Reading, Pennsylvania, in July 2007 when he got the call. The Philadelphia Phillies had traded him to the Reds. "I was on like the fourteenth hole, and they told me, 'You're pitching Wednesday in Huntsville [Alabama],'" he said. He had two days to pack up, say good-bye to his AA Reading Phillies teammates, and relocate. In baseball there are a lot of things you can't control. That may be why faith and superstition are so prevalent.

Matt's faith is in himself. A few weeks after his Major League debut last season, Matt was sent back down to the Bats. His wife, Kalee, said she was anxious, especially when a Reds game came on while they were out eating dinner. But Matt reacted calmly, she said, telling her, "I know I'll be back up."

He doesn't have any superstitions. Instead, he has Kalee, whose presence he says always makes him play better. She has yoga. On an off-day last season she got the word *Namaste* tattooed on her right wrist. It's a Sanskrit saying that translates roughly to "The spirit in me respects the spirit in you." Kalee's belief system is more of the general spiritual type than the organized-religion variety, but it serves the same purpose, helping her accept what she cannot control. And there is a lot of that, especially for someone who is used to the more organized and regimented life of a personal trainer. That was her career before she moved in with Matt. She tried to find more flexible employment last season, even landed a waitressing gig, but she quit it before she started when Matt was called up for his Major League debut.

This year his recall to the Reds came as less of a surprise. He's changed pitches a little bit, working on a cutter and a slider and trying to find the perfect mix with which to become more consistent, said Bats manager Rick Sweet. Matt continues to progress as far as consistency, his pitches, and refinement, said Sweet. So when Reds pitcher Aaron Harang was sidelined with back spasms, it made sense that Matt was the one recalled to the Reds.

What has been more surprising is how poorly the Bats are playing. The team hasn't had any losing streaks quite as bad as the nine-game one they suffered earlier in the season, but they haven't had many long winning ones, either. The wins they have had have been mostly low scoring and close.

The Reds are doing a lot better, and even look as if they might have a chance of making it to postseason play, something they haven't done in fifteen seasons. But it is only early July, and the postseason is still a long ways off. Also a long way off, at times, it seems, is the prospect of playing in the Major Leagues when you are sitting in the dugout of a AAA team. Just one phone call away, players like to say, but there is no guarantee that call will ever come.

Matt Maloney got it, once again, which is why he isn't here. Also missing from the scene is fellow pitcher Justin Lehr's son, Reed.

He never came. That's because Justin had Tommy John surgery at the end of May and is back now only to pay a visit. The procedure, named after a former Major League pitcher, involves using a tendon from somewhere else in the body to replace a ligament in the elbow and is credited with saving the careers of countless Major League players. It could do the same for Justin, or it could end his career. Which will happen is not something anyone will know until later. What is clear is that Justin won't be making it to the Majors this season; any promise he showed before the season began ended abruptly when he opted to have surgery. His season is over.

The surgery was a long time coming. Justin had been battling elbow trouble since 2006 and hadn't pitched without anti-inflammatory or pain medication since 2005. For a couple of years he took Voltaren, often used to help with arthritis, then Celebrex, also used for arthritis, osteoporosis, and acute pain. His seasons would start off okay, but once he got extended into a game a few innings, his elbow would start to bother him, letting him know he couldn't pitch without the drugs. So he kept taking them, and he kept pitching.

Two years ago an MRI of his elbow showed a partial ligament tear and several different calcifications on the same ligament where he had damaged it before. At the time, he says, he wasn't in a position to do anything about it. He had just signed with the Philadelphia Phillies as a Minor League free agent, and he didn't think surgery was an option if he wanted to keep his job. Instead, he did some rehabilitation—and kept pitching.

This time, it was different. Last off-season he stayed home, resting his arm instead of playing winter ball in Latin America.

But after his first start of the year he knew the rest hadn't been enough. As soon as he got extended in his pitch count, he lost stability and consistency. Not only was his velocity down, but so was his command of the ball. "I couldn't throw anything where I wanted to," he says. "It just wouldn't hold stable through my pitching delivery."

During one game in May he started strong. He allowed one run through five innings and then had a disastrous sixth inning, giving up four runs without retiring a single batter before he was removed. It was after that game that he asked to have another MRI.

The result wasn't a surprise. He knew the ligament was shot; he just didn't know he also had bone chips on the back of his elbow. Still, after more than a decade of full-season professional baseball—during four years of which he also played winter ball in the off-season—he knew he had it coming. If you pitch long enough, he says, odds are you're going to need medical intervention. "I don't know anybody my age that hasn't already had surgeries on something," he says. "I think it just comes with the nature of the business."

What he needed this time depended on what he wanted to do. To have the opportunity to pitch well for several more years, he needed Tommy John surgery. He also needed to have the bone chips removed. He could have done the latter and forgone the former and possibly continued pitching this season with the help of cortisone. But long term he knew that wasn't a solution. Without surgery he might have been able to play, but not at the level he knew he was capable of, and not for much longer.

The Reds organization had options as well. After the surgery they could have released him and let him finish his rehab at an outside clinic. Considering Justin's age, that is probably what would have been done if he had not pleaded his case, he says.

But he knew he didn't want to go through with the surgery if he wouldn't have a team to come back to the following year, so he argued to be kept on. His fear was that otherwise he would have been rehabilitated to the point of being able to throw off the mound in March, but without a team. "The likelihood of getting signed coming off Tommy John at my age, with my amount of big league time, probably is highly unlikely," he says. So that would have eliminated his 2011 season as well as the rest of his 2010 season. He also felt he would receive the best rehabilitation program at a Reds facility, where the staff is used to helping injured players regain their strength.

So after the surgery he returned home to Arizona and to rehabilitation at the Reds' Goodyear Ballpark in Goodyear, Arizona. The organization's Goodyear Reds Rookie League team plays there, and Reed goes with his father to hit in the batting cage while Justin rehabs. It is the ideal situation, considering what he was faced with. But, he admits, not all his friends see it that way, and some question his logic. In August he'll be thirty-three, with a year of rehabilitation ahead of him, which means he won't be playing again until he is almost thirty-four. Still, he believes if his arm is healthy, he could play another three or four years. And even if that is in AAA, or in Mexico, or wherever else the sport takes him, he wants those years.

He knows they may not be the best years financially, so to prepare he and Guia are already making changes. She got a job in education that starts at the beginning of the school year, and they traded in their GMC Yukon XL truck for a more fuel-efficient Chevy Malibu. With his trip to and from Goodyear each day coming to about ninety miles, the savings are noticeable. While in Goodyear he has also been able to help out on the coaching side. There is no question in his mind that he would like to coach someday. The only question is whether he could support his family coaching.

Family is something he has seen a lot of recently. He was even able to attend Reed's games. Reed's team made the playoffs, and for a few days Justin was at a baseball field daily, kind of like he usually is this time of year. Only the field was slightly smaller, and he was there as a spectator and not a participant. What he misses most about being away from the game, he says, is not the competing but the camaraderie. "You spend half your life in a baseball clubhouse, and all of a sudden you're not in one. It's different because you're used to being part of a team," he explains.

That is why he is back in the Bats' dugout this July weekend. He has come to hang out with his friends and teammates. Outfitted in his practice uniform, he doesn't look that different from the rest of them, until manager Rick Sweet spots him and asks to see his "zipper." Justin holds his arms out to the side, showing off his wing span and the scar that stretches down the inside of his right arm.

After the surgery he couldn't bend his arm to hold the phone to his ear. Now, almost six weeks later, he still can't mow the lawn with both hands, for fear the vibration might mess up the healing process. But in the dugout he doesn't mention any of this, instead joking about bench-press weights for post–Tommy John guys and teasing a younger player that maybe he can be an underachiever like Justin someday. With trainer Tomas Vera he jokes that he only came back to get a ride in Aroldis Chapman's Lamborghini. Then he runs onto the field to join his teammates for batting practice. He can't hit, but that doesn't mean he can't stand out there.

•

In the dugout one man remains behind, sitting by himself, dressed in sandals and a T-shirt, with bushy brows and a bit of scruff around his chin. In his hand is a book about the puzzle that is life and the fundamentals that can help you in life and in sports. He wrote it. Inside the book is a section on being coachable, broken down further into being coachable on the field, being coachable in life, and what the Bible says about being coachable. On the last entry Bob Bailey could tell you quite a bit. He is a retired Southern Baptist missionary based across the river in southern Indiana. He is in his seventies, and for the past twenty-seven years he has been a representative for Baseball Chapel with the Louisville team.

The international ministry has more than five hundred chapel leaders throughout professional baseball in both the Major and Minor Leagues.[1] In Louisville Bob reaches out to players, umpires, ushers, and concession workers. His two associates, both volunteers like Bob, hold ministries for the players' wives (and girlfriends) and the Hispanic players.

Bob conducts chapel services Sundays before home games. The players' service lasts about a half hour and is held in the family room where the players' families hang out during the game. Baseball Chapel assigns the topic, so players are assured of hearing a different service each week whether they are on the road or at home. But the ministry doesn't tell the leaders how to treat the topic, so Bob makes his own guide. This year's guide includes the one hundred top Christian baseball players of all time. When he isn't at the ballpark Bob has told reporters he enjoys water aerobics. He jokes that in old age his six-pack has turned into a keg.

Today is Friday, so he is here not for a sermon but for a discussion, this one on appreciating the experience, something he feels an athlete should understand. Bob comes to the ballpark nearly every day during home stretches but rarely catches an actual game; he leaves long before the first pitch. He arrives early in the afternoon to hang out in the clubhouse and be there should a player have a question. Sometimes they ask for a restaurant recommendation or directions. Other times they want to talk about relationships. Through the course of the season nearly every Louisville player will approach him with a question.

He listens to them all. His is a ministry of presence, but he is careful to differentiate himself from a chaplain, a role he considers similar to that of a counselor. He is neither; he'll provide council, but his primary purpose is evangelism, "to introduce people to Jesus." "I don't push," he says. "But I look for opportunities, because I think it solves a lot of problems some of these guys have."

There is a lot of anxiety in baseball, especially when someone is moved down a level. Bob tries to help players see the bigger picture, that while they have been moved down, they are still in the organization. It's all about perspective, something Bob believes faith helps you gain.

Attendance at his talks and services ranges from a few players to a dozen. Today he hopes to ask two of his regulars if they want to serve as chapel representatives, or liaisons between him and their teammates. Of the three representatives he's had this season, one made it to the bigs and the other two were released.

Tonight two players join him in the family room. They each take their own couch among Dora the Explorer toys and an old television. Toward the end of the discussion, heads bent in prayer, they ask God to help them enjoy and appreciate life now as it is happening, instead of down the line. Then they pray for a player's sick grandmother, another player's transition postbaseball, and safe travel for all. When they are finished Bob says good-bye, and the guys, ice wrapped around one of their shoulders, sandals on their feet, head to the locker room to dress for tonight's game against the Toledo Mud Hens.

In the dugout Scott Geiser and Ted Brown remain in their practice uniforms. The former is tall, thin, and, at thirty-eight, almost young enough looking to pass for a player. The latter is fifty-one and a little too round around the middle to still be playing. But they both are in the game, in their own way. They have lockers in the clubhouse, and every home game they are here for batting practice, helping warm up the guys by throwing pitches.

They aren't coaches. Scott works in marketing, Ted in health care. They do that during the day, the corporate gigs. In the afternoon they come here. They have been doing it for five years, and the perks aren't monetary—they aren't paid. Instead, the benefits are getting to know the players before they make it big and hearing the stories the older guys tell about their glory days.

Ted and Scott made it to college baseball. But after that their experience was pretty much limited to coaching high school baseball until they were approached about throwing batting practice for the Bats. It gives the coaches, all of whom have had long careers of their own, a little break. It gives Bob and Scott a chance to see the game up close and feel like they are a part of it. "I have a locker in the clubhouse, my own uniform and everything," says Scott. "I'm part of the family."

Elizabeth Namusoke Kizito is also part of the extended family. She sees the game from up in the stands and even then doesn't really see it. When customers ask her what is happening, half the time she doesn't even know who is playing. That's because she is busy balancing a basket of cookies on her head. It was her husband's idea. In her native Uganda that is how she grew up carrying things, and when she started selling cookies on a street corner decades ago, he told her she would attract more attention with the cookies on her head. It worked, and now all her cookies are labeled with a picture of a woman carrying a basket on her head.

Her website tells the story of how she was born under a banana tree and how her recipe comes from her father, who worked at a bakery in Africa. That's not entirely true; she was born under a tree, she insists, but the cookie recipe came from a magazine. Her father worked in a bakery, but growing up in Africa Elizabeth never tasted cookies, only biscuits. It was after coming to the United States as a teenager to study that she was introduced to chocolate chip cookies. She loved them so much she started making her own. In time her friends came to love them as well and convinced her to start selling her cookies, which is how her business, Kizito Cookies, came into being.

She has been selling her cookies at Bats games since the new stadium opened a decade ago. Tonight she arrives in a bright-yellow dress and tennis shoes, pulling a trolley stacked with boxes of cookies behind her. A woman at the stadium counting the cookies jokes she is counting the calories. Actually, she is counting how many Elizabeth brought in so they can get a cut of the profits. There are a lot, 420 tonight, each as large as a small child's face. Elizabeth will make it once around the stadium before running out. And she always runs out.

By the time she gets to usher Bobby "Perk" Perkins in section 107, she will probably be out. Perk is a sixty-three-year-old air force retiree who still has the neat look of a military man, with belted khaki shorts, short hair, and a dark tan. He has been the usher of 107 for as long as Elizabeth has been selling cookies. He chose this section down the right-field line because it's in the sun and by the women's bathroom. "Who doesn't like to sightsee?" he asks.

But what he is usually on the lookout for is not pretty women, but spectators having trouble locating their seats. The second he spots a lost soul he offers his assistance, leading them directly to their seat. He also takes their pictures when asked, answers their questions, and provides everything from batteries for their cameras to ice packs for their injuries. He keeps all the things he feels would be useful to a fan in a sports bag tucked in a corner toward the top of his section. "I've got sunscreen. I've got anything a fan needs, up to and including those little screwdrivers for sunglasses and first aid and instant ice packs," he says. There is a fan with an attached squirt bottle for hot days, gum-removal solution, Band-Aids, sunscreen . . . Perk continues to rattle off the list until he is distracted by the lost look of a couple approaching his section. He stops midsentence, offering, "Can I help you all?" Chances are he'll be able to. Maybe he helped the Bats as well, because they win the game 3–0. Or maybe all it took was a little faith.

8. Diminishing Returns

Chris Burke didn't plan to stay long in Louisville. He figured it was only a matter of time before he was back in the big leagues, where he belonged. Just like earlier in his career, when it had only been a matter of time until he would replace Craig Biggio and start at second base for the Houston Astros. Only just like then, things didn't go as anticipated. And now, like pitcher Justin Lehr, Chris's season has turned out far worse than he could have ever imagined. His response will take him down an entirely different path than the one his former teammate is pursuing.

A little before three thirty in the afternoon, Chris Burke is not at pregame batting practice. The former Major League player and Bats center fielder is not even in Louisville. Instead, he is on the road. But he is not traveling to an away game. The Bats have a home game tonight. Chris has a night class at Midway College, about an hour outside Louisville, and that is where he is headed.

It is late August, and if he keeps up his current schedule of night classes, he should be able to complete his degree in sports marketing by next spring. He hadn't planned on being able to finish so soon. He was supposed to be playing baseball. But in this sport, not unlike in life, what you envision and what happens are often two entirely different things. Knowing that doesn't make it any easier when the bombshell drops.

Chris signed with the Reds organization last winter, aware that if he didn't make the Majors he would be playing in Louisville, where he grew up and where he still lives. And that is where he ended up, despite having spent most of the past six years playing in the Majors. Chris was the number-ten overall draft pick out of the University of Tennessee in 2001 and played in the Majors for Houston, Arizona, and San Diego, most recently in 2009 for the San Diego Padres. While he would have liked a few more years in the Majors, there were advantages to being in Louisville. He was able to live at home, and his wife and two young children could come watch him play.

Then in late June the Reds signed outfielder Gary Matthews Jr. to a Minor League contract. It was clear someone was going to be moved. Chris figured he was safe. But his statistics told another story. He struggled in April, batting .211, and then raised his average to .252 in May. In June his average dropped to .238.

Gary played center field, and there were a lot of young prospects on the team. The Bats told Chris it was in his best interest, and the team's, if he was let go. That way he would have the opportunity to sign with somebody else. What they didn't know is that Chris didn't want to play anywhere else. "They did what they had to do," he says. "And then I did what I felt like was best for me and my family." He retired. There were offers from other AAA teams, but none enticing enough to uproot his family once again. Although he hadn't expected to be released, he had prepared for it and had already thought through his options. After ending his 2009 season in AAA with the Gwinnett Braves, he had decided that if he didn't get back to the big leagues in 2010, he would retire.

It was a reasonable decision, but a difficult one to make for a thirty-year-old athlete in the prime of his life with no injuries. Chris felt like he could do everything he used to do and more. But experience told him that wasn't all that mattered. He was now seen as a utility AAA player, someone who could play, and had played, every position but catcher and pitcher.

He could probably make it back to the bigs, but it might have taken him five or six stops along the way. He had seen it before, and he didn't want to go through it or put his family through it. He didn't want them to have to leave their friends and routines just so he could chase a dream he had already fulfilled. At this point Chris was just hanging on to that dream.

It was a good dream while it lasted. Highlights include helping lead his University of Tennessee team to the College World Series in 2001 and hitting a series-clinching home run for the Houston Astros in the 2005 National League Division Series. The Astros went on to reach the World Series that year. Chris went out as a career .239 Major League hitter and qualifies for a pension.

His one regret is that the Houston Astros never gave him a chance to start at second base, a position it seemed he was being groomed for at the beginning of his career. But after several years biding his time behind All-Star second baseman Craig Biggio, Chris was traded, and the Astros signed Kaz Matsui to play second base.

Chris isn't bitter so much as disappointed that he never got to see where starting at second base with the Astros would have taken him. Now he wants baseball to take him into coaching. Not the professional route. He was getting to the point where he felt physically ill before road trips, so he doesn't want to go through all the traveling and maneuvering that would entail. Instead, he wants to coach in college, where there isn't as much of a ladder to climb before you get to a spot where it is worth staying. Once he has a degree and is able to coach at the collegiate level, one thing he plans to share with his players is that every phase and stage along the way is great in and of itself.

Back in Louisville, sitting in the stands at Slugger Field, Kalee Maloney echoes Chris's thoughts. She has always talked about enjoying where you are, but feels she and Matt really grasped that this season. "We can be really happy. We don't have to be in the big leagues," she says.

But not everyone around them sees it that way. Friends and especially family want to know how Matt is handling not being in the Majors—not how he is doing in AAA. It's a new thing for the young couple, the parent dynamic in a baseball player's life. But it is one Kalee believes is not uncommon. Parents often invest a lot of energy, time, and money in their sons' baseball dreams. They may forget to inquire about the other aspects of their athletes' lives.

Last season when it looked as if then Bats first baseman Kevin Barker's baseball career might be coming to an end, his father, Bill Barker, was as lost as Kevin. Since Kevin was five years old, Bill said, he and his wife, Anna, had focused on Kevin's baseball. They signed Kevin up for baseball camps when he was a kid, and when he was in college they packed up the car almost every spring weekend and headed to wherever Kevin's team was playing. Later Bill would visit Kevin in the countless little towns he played in as he worked his way up the Minor League ladder. Bill would rent and furnish an apartment for Kevin while Kevin was still at spring training so it would be ready when Kevin arrived. Bill and Anna have kept every newspaper clipping there is on their son's baseball career. If that ends, Bill wondered, "what are we going to do? It's been our life for all of these years too," he said.

This season Kalee says Matt became frustrated because he felt his parents didn't seem to ask about any aspect of his life besides baseball. He was hurt that it seemed to him as if they called and texted him only when he pitched well, she says. And it wasn't just Matt's parents. This season Kalee's family, which usually doesn't pay much attention to baseball, became very involved. Kalee even stopped talking to her father briefly when he wouldn't stop talking about Matt's career. She wanted her father to understand there are other aspects to their lives and that even though Matt spent most of the season in AAA, they are happy. And they have been in good company, with Matt's close friend and Reds pitcher Daniel Ray Herrera spending a lot of the season with them in AAA.

Daniel may be enjoying himself a little too much. In late July the diminutive pitcher was charged with public intoxication across the river in Indiana. He was arrested around four o'clock on a Wednesday morning and released later that same day. It is relatively rare these days for players like Daniel, savvy to the ways of the media and careful to maintain their image, to get caught misbehaving in public. Needless to say, the media had a field day, with newspapers picking up the story of the drunken ballplayer and blogs posting Daniel's somber mug shot.

Liability and media relation departments long ago put an end to the days when reporters could ride the bus with players and watch women fall all over them after games. Being a female, it was unlikely I would be able to see any of that anyway. But there was another way I could learn about the players, an opening into their lives often overlooked. I got to know their wives and girlfriends, the women who stood by them through the ups and downs and were eager to let others into their sometimes lonely lives. Like many male athletes, Matt didn't talk about emotions much. It was Kalee who shared details like the newly challenging parental dynamic and the negotiations about living arrangements, the fact that all Matt's time in AAA meant the Maloneys would be doing what Matt wanted this off-season—staying put. They agreed before the season started that if Matt spent most of the season in the Majors, making Major League money, they would spend the off-season in Austin, Texas, like last year. But without the big league bucks to help them make the move, they decided to stay in Louisville and started looking for a cozier place.

They found one two doors down from their favorite breakfast eatery on one of the city's more hip streets. It is a duplex with a fenced-in yard for their dogs and a patio to grill out on. But most important, it is in Louisville, the city Matt has come to consider home. They will make a few trips during the off-season, to Austin to visit friends and to nearby Columbus for Ohio State football games. Matt is a huge Ohio State fan and already has tickets to at least one game.

Then there is Venezuela, where Matt may end up playing winter ball. He doesn't really want to go, would prefer to rest, but if playing for a month in Venezuela means he doesn't have to get a job for the rest of the off-season, that is pretty enticing. Kalee thought about going with him until Matt told her she wouldn't be able to leave the hotel without a bodyguard because it is so dangerous. In August a woman playing in the Women's Baseball World Cup there was hit in the leg by a stray bullet during a game. Kalee is now leaning toward visiting Matt for a week and spending the rest of the time in Louisville.

She attended a lot of home games this season, and even though the weather is cooling now, she is still in the habit of bringing a towel to sit on so she doesn't stick to the seats. It is a routine she developed during the hundred-plus-degree weather that beat down on the region for much of July and August. She also keeps a fan in her purse, a gift from the fiancée of one of Matt's teammates.

Kalee has always been close with several of the girlfriends and wives of other players, but this year she has become even closer. At the beginning of the season she talked about not being able to relate to some of the other wives and girlfriends, but now she talks about not being able to relate to her old friends back home in Sandusky. During a trip home earlier this season, her closest friends were different, she says: "Just colder, didn't really ask about me."

In the dugout her husband echoes her affection for a season that hasn't turned out as he would have liked. He is happy with how he has performed, with three wins and one loss and a 1.00 ERA in four games in July. And he is pretty confident he'll get called up in September when the big league rosters expand to forty players. He feels he can help the team as they continue to make their playoff push and that he proved that during his time with the Reds in July. He was up for only a little more than a week, but playing on a team that actually had a chance of making it to the postseason was an experience he won't soon forget. "It's a different atmosphere than I've ever been in, and it makes you really hungry to get back there and play in that kind of atmosphere," he says.

Bats pitching coach Ted Power, who spent about half of his thirteen-year Major League pitching career with the Reds, says

Matt pitched well when he was up in the Majors, represented himself well, and after a very solid year should look forward to returning to the Majors very shortly. Just how soon isn't a question Ted can answer. He isn't up there. He is in the Minors, where, until this season, he wasn't even allowed to grow facial hair while in the Reds organization. Now that the rules have changed, he has a little salt-and-pepper-sprinkled stubble on his chin. But for years he kept himself clean shaven. He knows how the system works, and so does Matt. Matt's "pretty mature. He understands the situation," says Ted. He understands there is simply no room for him with the pitching-rich Reds right now.

Then there is Aroldis Chapman, the Cuban superstar. In late June the Bats moved him to the bullpen because the Reds didn't need any starters and Aroldis was struggling as a starter. Making him a relief pitcher was an experiment that turned out tremendously well. "I don't think anybody dreamed that his command would get so much better. And his velocity stays consistent," says Ted.

Instead of just rearing back and throwing the ball as hard as he can, Aroldis now has more control over his delivery. He could always throw, better than anyone Ted had ever seen. Still, his limited knowledge of the game has meant a huge amount of extra work for the coaching staff, says manager Rick Sweet. Aroldis came to the Bats with a tremendous arm, but no idea about the game of baseball itself. He had to be taught everything, says Rick, "covering first base, backing up bases, knowing game strategy, game situation, how to set up hitters," the kind of things that are taught in high school, college, and the lower levels of the Minors, but not in AAA. Bats president Gary Ulmer sees it a little differently. Having Aroldis in Louisville allowed fans to watch a level of talent they've probably never seen before and may never see again.

The season is winding down now. Children are back in school and the stands are relatively empty, but Gary still makes his rounds at the ballpark. He keeps a container of crunchy peanut butter under his desk for the long days and plenty of dress shirts and polo shirts on the back of his office door for all the different roles he juggles at the ballpark and away. He keeps his golf shoes in the trunk of his car for when the season ends and he has time to sneak out early on Friday afternoons.

While he plans to make some changes next year, like holding games earlier on school nights, overall the 2010 season turned out better than Gary expected in what continues to be a weak economy. Season tickets and corporate sponsorships haven't necessarily been up, but walk-up traffic has been strong, probably a little better than the past couple of years, especially in the second half of the season when the Bats started racking up wins—eleven in a row in late July and early August. While a beautiful summer night has more of an effect on attendance than a winning or losing team, he says, the Bats' exceptional turn from dismal to strong in about a six-week period definitely hasn't hurt.

Now that they are headed for the playoffs, it is even more exciting. Except that the Reds are making a playoff push too, which means the big league team will probably call up some of the Bats' best players in September. But Gary isn't complaining. "We understand our role," he says. "And that is that we're here for the Reds."

It may be hard, he says, but you're kidding yourself if you think that's not the way it should be. And that's the way it ends. On September 1 the Bats lose a catcher, a pitcher, and a first baseman to the Reds. Two days later they lose two more pitchers, including Matt Maloney.

Aroldis went earlier. On August 31 the Cuban made his Major League debut against the Milwaukee Brewers. He pitched a perfect inning, facing three batters and hitting 102 on the radar gun. Tomas Vera finally made it to the bigs—but only to help Aroldis.

9. The Star Who Almost Landed in Louisville

In the end, after a disappointing early season, the Bats went on to greatness, as expected. They won their third straight International League West Division title, before being eliminated in the first round of the playoffs by the Durham Bulls. The same cannot be said of utility player Chris Burke and pitchers Matt Maloney and Justin Lehr. Justin got injured, Chris was released, and Maloney didn't spend nearly as much time in the Majors as he had hoped.

It is a theme Mary E. Barney knows well—disappointment. In her day the manager broke the news when players were released, traded, or reassigned, but Mary was the one who signed the paperwork. She remembers well the one occasion she had to do the talking. The team had a day off, so she was in charge of telling a pitcher he was being sent down. The only problem was he was Spanish speaking, and so she had to get a bilingual player to explain to him what was going on. "I didn't want him to sign something that he didn't know what the consequences were of him signing that," she says.

He took it okay, she says. She has no idea how Matt, Justin, or Chris took their disappointments this season. It's been a while since she's been to a Bats game, and she doesn't know the players anymore. But she knows Gary Ulmer, remembers when he was hired to sell tickets along with a bunch of other youngsters. Back then the sales staff dressed in blue blazers emblazoned with the team logo and drove around in cars provided by Ford Motor Company, which has had a plant in Louisville since 1955.

She knows Gary's father, Dan, even better. Her husband, Walter, was in advertising and worked with Dan's bank when the whole "bring baseball back to Louisville" campaign got under way in the early 1980s. She still has a bumper sticker with the slogan Walter developed—"Baseball . . . a great catch for Louisville." And when it worked and A. Ray Smith decided to move his Redbirds from Springfield, Illinois, to Louisville in 1981, Walter hired on to provide advertising for the team.

Mary's hiring was a little less conventional. As the mother of five, most of her baseball experience was with Little League. She is from Chicago originally, and Walter always teased that the only time she ironed was when she was watching the Chicago Cubs on television. Then baseball was brought back to Louisville, and Mary ended up in the inner circle, thanks to her husband's role.

At a dinner following the press conference at which A. Ray announced he was moving his team to Louisville, she spent the night talking baseball with the guys. Next thing she knew A. Ray had invited her to breakfast at his hotel. When she showed up at his suite, two phones were ringing. He asked her if she could answer a phone. She replied, "What woman can't?" and picked up a line. That was her first day on the job. "I never talked the job, I never talked salary, I never talked anything," she says. "I picked up one phone, he picked up the other phone, and that was my first day."

She started as a receptionist, moved up to secretary, and ended twenty-five years later as director of baseball operations. Along the way she won numerous awards, including Rawlings Woman Executive of the Year for all of professional baseball in 2000 and the George M. Trautman Award, recognizing her for outstanding service to Minor League Baseball in 1992.

There weren't a lot of women in baseball front offices back then, and Mary thinks one reason she was able to get along so well was because she respected what she calls "the code of silence." It is a code she observed when staff members would go out to dinner after games and talk about personal matters. She knew never to share the things she heard at those gatherings with anyone else. She learned not to seat the wives and girlfriends in the same area of the stadium.

Now, at seventy, dressed in workout clothes, her white hair pulled back in a loose bun, Mary flips through a scrapbook filled with photos. A. Ray Smith liked to entertain the greats, and she met quite a few of them. There she is with longtime Major League Baseball announcer George Grande pinching her cheek; there she is leaning her head in next to that of Baseball Hall of Famer Ernie Banks. In other photos she can be seen with former New York Yankees manager Billy Martin and longtime Yankees pitcher Whitey Ford. She never asked for their autographs, didn't think it was appropriate.

But one time she got one anyway. She was sitting next to New York Yankees great and Hall of Famer Mickey Mantle one night, and even though she didn't ask for it, Mickey gave her an autograph—on her thigh. She covers her mouth in embarrassment and a little pride as she points to a photo in her album. In the picture you can see that Mickey turned the mole on her leg into a sun, and then signed his name below. It took three days to wash it off.

In some ways, the players were like her children, and many even called her "Mom." One time a young pitcher, Todd Worrell, took batting practice in his socks. Mary found out why later when he showed up in her office with a pair of pink cleats. It was opening night 1983, and Todd was the team's starting pitcher. He had one pair of cleats, the pink ones. Their red coloring had faded during the rainy spring. Mary carried the cleats to a cobbler, had them shined red, and returned in time for Todd to wear them in the home opener.

She took things even further with another Louisville player, Tracy Woodson, who suffered a concussion after colliding with a player during a playoff game in Indianapolis. The Redbirds lost the game, eliminating them from the playoffs and thus ending their season. Everyone was eager to get home, but the doctors ordered Tracy to spend the night in Indianapolis. He could leave the hospital, but not the city. He also had to be woken every two hours throughout the night. So Mary took him back to the hotel where they had been staying and settled down to spend the night reading a book and drinking a lot of Coke. She woke him every two hours and took him back to Louisville the next day.

Back at the ballpark, Mary's role included a little of everything, from taking care of travel arrangements and ordering office supplies to answering middle-of-the-night phone calls from players asking where they should take their sick children. When Hall of Famer Satchel Paige was scheduled to join the team as vice president, she found him an apartment. She talked to him in June 1982, the day before he was scheduled to come to Louisville for his new job. That was also the day before he died.

She still has a small stack of the Redbirds' business cards they made for him, a reminder of the star that almost landed in Louisville. They are more off-white than white now and list no fax number, e-mail address, website, or cell phone number, just a street address and phone number. But on the back there is something else, Satchel's rules for the good life:

Avoid fried foods cause they angers up the blood.
If your stomach disputes you, lay down and pacify it with cool thoughts.
Keep the juices flowin' by janglin' 'round gently as you move.
Go very light on vices such as carryin' on in society. The social ramble
    just ain't restful.
Avoid runnin' at all times.
Don't ever look back. Somethin' might be gainin'.

While Satchel never made it to Louisville for the Redbirds job, he was in town before, in 1941 for an exhibition game, when he was still playing. Louisville's baseball history stretches back to the game's early days. In 1875 Louisville was the setting for talks on establishing the National League. It was supposed to be a "respectable" league, without the gambling and other unsavory habits that haunted the sport, but Louisville's team had some gambling problems of their own, and they were forced to drop out of the league after the 1877 season.[1]

They rejoined the Major Leagues in 1882 with the American Association. One of the Louisville players to make his mark on the town during this time was Pete Browning, whose lifetime batting average of .341 is the eleventh highest in Major League history.[2] His hitting earned him the nickname the "Louisville

Slugger," a name that has stayed in the city due to the bats that bear that trademark.

The story behind the bats is said to be that John Andrew "Bud" Hillerich was working at his father's Louisville woodworking business when he made a bat in 1884. He gave this bat to Pete after Pete broke one of his own. Pete was in a slump, but after using the new bat he got several hits. Bud convinced his father to have the company take on bat making. The business, Hillerich & Bradsby Company, trademarked the bat the Louisville Slugger in 1894.[3] Today the Slugger is the official bat of Major League Baseball.

Louisville played in the National League from 1892 to 1899, when the league downsized and Louisville was one of the teams dropped. And so ended Louisville's Major League experience, a time during which six future members of the Baseball Hall of Fame played here: Hughey Jennings, Fred Clarke, Dan Brouthers, Jimmy Collins, Honus Wagner, and Rube Waddell.[4]

In 1902 Louisville joined a new baseball league, the American Association—not to be confused with the former Major League one—and the Minor Leagues. It might not have been the Majors, but the city embraced it just the same. Fans frequented one shortcut to an early ballpark so often that it was renamed Baseball Alley.

The relationship lasted, allowing plenty more legends to leave their mark on the city, among them Harold "Pee Wee" Reese. Pee Wee, who attended high school in Louisville, signed with Louisville in 1938 and after retiring from the game worked with Louisville Slugger. He was elected to the Baseball Hall of Fame in 1984 and has a street named after him in his hometown. There were others who left their mark or went on to the Hall of Fame: player-manager Joe McCarthy, Kentucky native Earle Combs, and second baseman Billy Herman among them.

Then, in the 1950s, attendance at Minor League Baseball games around the country started to drop, and for about five years in the 1960s Louisville was without a Minor League team. From 1972 to 1981 they again found themselves without a team. That's when A. Ray Smith agreed to bring his AAA farm team for the St. Louis Cardinals to town. Since then professional baseball seems to be back in Louisville for good, or at least the foreseeable future.

In 1998 the team became affiliated with the Milwaukee Brewers and changed their name to the RiverBats, which was later shortened to the Bats. In 2000 the team joined the Cincinnati Reds' farm system. Today the team's Most Valuable Player award is named for Mary E. Barney. She may not know the player whom it will go to this year, but she knows whoever gets it will deserve it. All of them do. The Minor League life is a tough one, and when she was still working for the team she used to try to explain this to fans who called in to complain that a ballplayer hadn't given them an autograph. Mary would tell the callers that it was like before they went into a business meeting and were concentrating and distracted; the same was true of ballplayers before a game. If a player didn't give an autograph, she would explain, it wasn't because they were being rude, but because they were concentrating on the job ahead. "To you it's a game," she would tell callers, "but to them it's their job."

10. (*Top*) Louisville Bats mascot Buddy Bat and pitcher Matt Maloney enjoy a laugh. By James Calvert.

11. Louisville Bats president Gary Ulmer holds up some of the spare clothes he keeps in his office. By James Calvert.

12. (*Above*) Louisville Bats usher Bobby "Perk" Perkins keeps all the things a fan might need, from batteries to ice packs, in a bag in his section. By James Calvert.

13. (*Opposite*) Kalee Maloney, wife of Louisville Bats pitcher Matt Maloney, watches the game from the stands. By James Calvert.

14. Cotton candy at a Louisville Bats
game. By James Calvert.

Part 3
Bowling Green Hot Rods:
The Business of Baseball

10. America's Other Pastime

Boys hitting a ball in the neighborhood, grown men playing catch with their sons, summer nights spent in the stands watching a game as endless as the season—those are the kind of scenes that made baseball America's pastime. Endless promotions, signing bonuses, and agents are the kind of things that have transformed the sport into a business. It's nothing new really; after all this is America, and our other pastime is making money. But each year the business part seems to get a little bigger and the sport part a little smaller, further widening the gulf between the players and the public.

Today, even in the Minors, it is hard for a writer to ride the team bus. Liability is the reason given—insurance covers the team and staff on bus rides but not outsiders. Getting to the players requires the intermediary of a press officer. The athletes' words are spoken carefully, no doubt practiced for just such an occasion. They want to advance up the baseball ladder, and they know image is important. They have agents, they have media handlers, and sometimes it seems they are the property of the club before they are people. Stick around long enough and you get past this, but the business part is always there, especially in the Minors, and in Bowling Green I decided to make it the focus. The Bowling Green Hot Rods offered the perfect example, because they were so new. Everything about the team was still being built.

Tom Gauthier is the man in charge of broadcasting their image, plus a host of other things, especially in the off-season, when, for obvious reasons, the sport aspect is completely over-shadowed by the business one. Working in sales is not what Tom is here to do. He is the guy who gives fans listening on the radio a play-by-play account of each game. He also handles the media. It can be tricky at times, balancing interview requests and broadcasting duties. But at least those are in his job title. Selling seats and advertisements is not.

But it is seventy-six days until the Bowling Green Hot Rods play their first game of the 2010 season, and as part of the Hot Rods' front-office staff, that's what you do. And, on this January afternoon, so is greeting guests. That job is Tom's by default: his office is closest to the front door, and the receptionist recently left for a job with big-time local employer Fruit of the Loom. In Bowling Green, Kentucky, a city of about fifty-six thousand whose name is a mystery to even some of its residents, working for the underwear giant is a sought-after position. Answering phones at the ballpark office and playing the team mascot are not.

How Tom ended up taking on the latter and playing Axel the Bear isn't clear, at least at first. Last Saturday he took his act to the nearby Corvette museum. Tom bikes to work daily and is still a few years shy of his ten-year college reunion, but after a morning spent at the gym, he found it hard to keep up with the museum announcer's requests. "The guy killed me," says Tom, "song after song wanting Axel to dance."

Tom is a sports broadcaster by trade, a baseball man by obsession, and a mascot by size. He learned the basics of mascot behavior the summer of 2008 when he was an assistant radio broadcaster with the AA Portland Sea Dogs in Portland, Maine. He was given a thirty-minute tutorial on how to walk, move, and generally act like Slugger the Sea Dog.

There was no such training for Axel. But then Axel has been around for only a year, as have the Hot Rods, a Class-A team for the Tampa Bay Rays. Professional baseball has never been a big part of Bowling Green's history; the big sports in town are usually played at Western Kentucky University, located in the center of town. But the ballpark is a major part of a downtown redevelopment district that will eventually include a performing arts center, parking garage, hotels, and other new businesses.

Bowling Green will always be a sleepy sideshow compared to nearby Nashville, but that hasn't stopped Kentucky's fourth-largest city from trying to create its own attractions. Before baseball its biggest coup was the Corvette assembly plant General Motors opened in 1981. If you are in Kentucky and you aren't part of Appalachia and aren't Louisville or Lexington, you have to have something, and the distinction of being the provincial capital of the Confederate government of Kentucky doesn't cut it these days. Corvettes, on the other hand, do, which is why the city has embraced the National Corvette Museum, which went up in 1994 and where Tom, as Axel, had the pleasure of dancing recently.

Ah, yes, the mascot. Last season a local college student took on the role of Axel, a part that proved more challenging than you might imagine. Without going into too much detail, let's just say when you lose your bear head, it isn't as simple as just picking it up and putting it on again, explains Tom. There are children who believe the bear is real, and if you are that bear, you'd better keep them believing. Again, the image thing. Tom was reluctant to even tell me this harmless story for fear it might make the staff look unprofessional.

A quick-witted jokester, Tom takes baseball incredibly seriously, said his wife, Judy Gauthier. If he messes up on air, she will be sure to hear about it later that night. A lifelong Red Sox fan, Tom claimed he would never even date a Yankees fan. Then he married one. Growing up in New York City, Judy didn't just say she was a fan; she backed it up by attending the games and knowing exactly who was on the team. That ended when she married Tom and he became a baseball broadcaster. "It's like I don't even like baseball anymore," said Judy, a travel buyer. "I'm so sick of baseball, sick of hearing about baseball. I'm sick of seeing baseball. I can't even tell you who is on the Yankees anymore because, literally, ESPN comes on and I shut it off."

Her husband doesn't have the same problem. If Judy misses his broadcast and asks him who won the game, he goes into detail, giving her a play-by-play of what happened. "I'll pretend like I'm listening, but I just wanted to know the score. I just wanted to know if they won," she said.

Although the season exhausts Tom, she said by January he is antsy for it to begin again. It is a restlessness he shares with the rest of the front-office staff.

Back at the ballpark a voice calls from the hallway, "Hey, folks, 4:30." Heads pop out of office doors, and a dozen or so khaki-clad employees, mostly male, make their way toward the couches in the back of the Hot Rods' front office. If the players were the high school jocks, the Hot Rods' front-office staff seems to be composed of class clowns and trivia geeks.

Greg Coleman stands to the side of a dry-erase board, a Diet Coke and pad of paper at the ready. After an update on the Diet Coke situation, key to Greg's and Tom's existence, Greg gets down to business. Unlike Tom, who is almost as new to baseball management as baseball is to Bowling Green, Greg has been with baseball more than a dozen years. As the assistant front-office general manager of sales, Greg is like an enthusiastic camp counselor rallying his campers before the group talent contest.

There is still more than a week left in January, but Greg announces that the sales team has already reached their goal of sponsorship numbers for the month. A short burst of applause is followed by Greg's announcement that there are still big advertising sales numbers to fill in February and March.

But this week's meeting is not about numbers. It's about ideas. For those who still think Minor League Baseball is about home runs and stolen bases, listen carefully to the presidents and front-office general managers of Minor League teams. They refer to the game not as a sport, but as family entertainment. Their financial success comes not from the team's performance, but from attendance numbers and advertising, two things that don't seem to have a lot to do with the actual playing of baseball.

While the players are entertaining the fans who are there to watch the game, the sales team has to find a way to attract a larger audience. And that's how you end up with "Toy Hall of Fame" and "Hootie Palooza," the first two ideas Greg wants to flesh out. Greg admits that Hootie Palooza, a tribute to the '90s rock band Hootie and the Blowfish and their lead singer, Darius Rucker, would have been more relevant a decade and a half ago. "But that's the fun about it," he says.

He isn't joking. When you have to come up with seventy promotions a year, one for each home game, cheesy and dated aren't always bad. And this one isn't as out there as it sounds. Although there is no obvious connection between the Hot Rods and the rock band, Greg has his reasons for suggesting a "Hootie Palooza" promotion. It is a catchy title, many people know the band's songs, and in addition to being the date of one of their home games, May 13 happens to be the birthday of Darius Rucker. It also happens that on his birthday last year, Darius asked that people donate to a needy school instead of giving him gifts. This may or may not help explain why Greg thought playing the band's music and generally having fun with the whole Hootie thing, maybe even getting Darius to come and have people give something to a charity, would make a good game-day promotion. "Some of you were alive when their music actually came out, so I'd like to at least have a discussion [about] what can be tied into that night besides the obvious," Greg says. Song titles are blurted out, and production manager and official meeting scribe Atlee McHeffey, who probably was not old enough to listen to rock when the band was popular, writes them on the board—"Hold My Hand," "Only Wanna Be with You," "Time."

"Isn't blowfish, like, a poisonous delicacy in Japan or something?" asks front-office general manager Brad Taylor. "Yeah, let's have a blowfish-eating contest." Other suggestions include a chicken wing–eating contest, something goatee oriented in honor of Rucker's penchant for facial hair, and a Miami Dolphins connection because Darius is a Dolphins fan. After that it gets even more off track, with comments about Tom's inferior video library. That is about when president Rick Brenner rolls his chair into the room and suggests a hand-holding contest. Something about handing out prizes to the couple who holds hands the longest appeals to the staff, and a new idea-shouting session is set in motion. Someone suggests having a local jewelry store sponsor the contest, offering a ring as a prize. To keep things from getting too serious, Rick throws in a jibe about a "Review Your Vows Night" featuring a celebrity whose serial cheating has made recent tabloid fodder. Logically, they move on to toys from there.

The toy promotion is a sort of tribute to toys that stand the test of time, and head of operations Ken Clary seems to be its main backer. "I have a Hook coloring contest with crayons, you know, do the black-and-white Hook, [and] just have them color it in," he says. "I mean, not Hook, Axel. Hook was in Columbus." Wrong mascot, right team. Columbus, Georgia, was where the team was before moving to Bowling Green. Ken is one of the few Columbus employees still on board. The team got bought and moved not because there weren't baseball fans in Columbus, but because Bowling Green offered a new ballpark and other enticements. Ken has been in the sport twenty years, and sometimes the teams he has worked with blur together.

Atlee, on the other hand, hasn't been around long enough to know that a "Barbie of Kentucky" beauty contest as part of the toy tribute is not an option. Greg explains why: "I don't think you can effectively utilize the trademark in that way. If I bought something, it's up to me if I want to give it away in that way. However, if I brand something under a registered trademark, I can't really do that."

It isn't clear that Atlee understands, but it is clear the beauty contest is off the table. And with that they move on to comic books, a possible promotion for the end of a thirteen-day home stretch. "We could do like if the Hot Rods score thirteen runs, the fans get something," suggests Tom.

"Is that for the whole home stretch?" asks Brad.

They get a little more leverage out of the comic book thing before opening the discussion up to other suggestions for promotions. Atlee, having not learned from the Barbie idea, is quick to offer another female-friendly idea—a Youth Sports Mom Day. "Can you rephrase that?" asks Greg.

Atlee pauses amid the laughter, trying to figure out how to get off the hook for unintentionally promoting teenage motherhood. "Youth Sports Night Ode to Mom, something like that," he says.

But no one is really listening anymore; they are having too much fun mocking Atlee, one of their newer members. When they start ribbing him about his name, Atlee makes another mistake. Needless to say, he probably realized the minute it was out of his mouth that revealing the "English meaning" of his name was not a good idea. Definitely not, especially considering he believes it to be "meadow."

And on that note, the meeting adjourns. After almost everyone else has gone home for the night, president Rick Brenner explains that what just occurred is one of the biggest differences between Minor and Major League Baseball. Down here, managing a baseball team is more about business than sports. "I often joke that for us, clean restrooms and a friendly staff are almost as important, if not as important, as a good shortstop," he says. That's because, in the Minors, there is no control over players. Who the team gets, and for how long, is decided by its Major League affiliate.

Rick may have played baseball at Plymouth State University in New Hampshire, but it was his childhood penchant for putting on backyard plays and haunted houses that really decided his future. During college he paid the bills by managing bar bands. Afterward he planned to work in ice hockey. But then his father got sick, and somehow he ended up taking an unpaid internship closer to home in New Jersey. He didn't even know Minor League Baseball existed when he went to work for the AA Trenton Thunder. Five and a half years later he was front-office general manager.

Now he serves as president of both the Hot Rods and the AA New Hampshire Fisher Cats, both owned by his boss, Art Solomon. Before they became the Hot Rods they were the Columbus Catfish. Solomon was looking to own another team, and Bowling Green was building a new ballpark, and that is how the Columbus Catfish morphed into the Bowling Green Hot Rods. It happens all the time. But it was the first time Rick had to build things from scratch. The only experience he had that came close was when he started at Trenton three months before they were supposed to move into a new stadium. Back then he wasn't even paid, and now he was in charge. And he had to do everything. "When we started we had nothing," he says. "I remember I was here, Brad [Taylor] wasn't even hired yet, we had one intern on staff, and we went to Staples and bought paper clips, a small printer, and a notebook. And the Chamber [of Commerce] was kind enough to lend us some office space, and off we went."

General manager Brad Taylor came along not long after. He had worked with Rick in Trenton, and when he heard Rick and Art might be starting a team in Kentucky, where both he and his wife have family, he got in touch. It wasn't just the location he liked. He was intrigued by the idea of working with a new team. "I've always wanted to have an opportunity to help with a start-up team from scratch," he explains. "To see the stadium get built, to create a brand and a look and a logo from the ground up and try something new. And this was my opportunity." His opportunity to play baseball was short-lived. He played second base for Randolph-Macon College in Ashland, Virginia, but never went professional. "Oh, I thought about it," he says. "Nobody else did." He is good-humored about his athleticism, or lack thereof. "I was a five-foot-eight kid that could run a little bit, and I couldn't hit and I couldn't throw. And apparently those two things are quite important to be a professional baseball player."

But they aren't necessary to manage a professional baseball team from the office side of things. And neither is wearing a suit and tie, which is good, because when Brad was hired in July 2008, the stadium was nothing more than a pile of dirt. He made sales calls on his cell phone sitting on a paint bucket because there was no phone or furniture in the borrowed office where he set up. "Something about it was pretty pure," he says.

Organic, another word he uses to describe that time, is probably more accurate. In the off-season, while the stadium was being built, Brad kept hearing how little it rains and snows in western Kentucky. What he saw was snow and so much rain that it penetrated the roof of the old building they were working in. "At the time the front room was our little makeshift merchandise room because it faced the street front, and we had to scramble to take ceiling tiles down, move merchandise, and move the computers that were up there," he recalls.

But it was building the company structure, not building the stadium and office, that really proved challenging. So many things you never think of in a company—like vacation policy, community initiative—it all had to be put on paper. And it was all being embarked on in a place that had not had a baseball team in recent history. There were no season-ticket holders to call, so they opened up a phone book, looked in their Chamber of Commerce directory, and started calling the biggest employers in town.

Their timing wasn't great. The country was in the midst of one of the biggest recessions it had seen in decades, and they were selling for the fourth quarter of 2008 and first quarter of 2009 at a time when some businesses had already set their budgets for those quarters. And they were selling something that did not yet exist. They couldn't show potential advertisers what their scoreboard sign would look like because there was no scoreboard. "I could come show people a nice pile of dirt, not quite a stadium yet," says Brad.

And while there were a lot of baseball fans who had worked hard to bring the team to town, there were also quite a few skeptics. Brad remembers one of them telling him he'd never get five hundred people to a game. "And I said, 'Really, five hundred people, you don't think we can get five hundred people to a game?'" recalls Brad. The guy didn't, not in his city, not in Bowling Green, so Brad promised to have at least three thousand people at opening night or he'd quit. It wasn't much of a threat; he knew if there weren't that many, he'd be fired anyway.

To build a fan base he had to drum up excitement, and one way he did that was by holding a name-the-team contest that drew more than one thousand different team names. There were the car-themed names: Sparkplugs, Turbos, and Speedsters, all playing off Bowling Green's being home of the Corvette. There were what Brad calls the "doozies," the Bluegills and Mammoths. And then there was the runner-up, the Cave Shrimp, which proved so popular the Hot Rods made a promotion out of it called "What Could've Been Night." For one night they looked at what would have happened if certain things in history had turned out differently, including the name of the team. They put Cave Shrimp on the scoreboard, gave out Cave Shrimp T-shirts, and created player head shots with a Cave Shrimp logo. The idea won them the title of Best Minor League Promotion of 2009.

What could have been was a little scarier before the season started. The players arrived in early April and had to dress in a hotel because the clubhouse wasn't complete. Opening day was April 17. The first day Brad was allowed in the stadium without a hard hat was April 15. The first day he and the rest of the office staff were allowed in to get things ready was April 16. "It was nerve-racking because a lot of what we do is predicated around things being set up like computer systems, graphic animations for scoreboards, stereo, speaker, just all kind of stuff," says Brad.

Even after the season started and the stadium opened, the front-office staff was going between a temporary ticket office and their old office building until the second week in July, when their on-site offices were complete. None of that mattered to Brad on opening night. He felt calm. Maybe it was from the utter exhaustion of getting everything ready, spending nights sleeping in the office, setting things up until the very last minute. Whatever it was, a feeling that everything was going to be great came over him. And it was. Almost seven thousand people showed up. Brad jokingly thanked them for saving his job.

11. The Start-Up Sprint

In only their second year, the Hot Rods' front-office staff has the youth, energy, and excitement of an Internet start-up. Working in Minor League Baseball with its long summer days, laid-back dress code, and focus on entertainment tends to attract the young and adventuresome, and the newness of the situation in Bowling Green only enhances that. There is no reputation or tradition to uphold here; the Hot Rods are making it up as they go along. It takes guts and enthusiasm to take a job with a team that barely exists. The Hot Rods' staff is gutsy and lively, and they know how to enjoy life in a way only those who give everything to a company they know may not exist in a year can.

In the press box at Bowling Green Ballpark broadcaster Tom Gauthier talks as fast as he moves, which is fast. The kind of fast you get when you are running on adrenaline and not rest. It's a hot Friday afternoon in mid-June, and Tom and the team have been back in Bowling Green maybe six hours. They left two Monday mornings ago for Wisconsin and rolled into Bowling Green around six this morning, after an eight-hour drive following last night's game in Lansing.

Although Tom drove his own vehicle this time, his usual mode of transportation is the team bus, with its reclining chairs and satellite television. As a team they've watched professional basketball and Sunday-night baseball on the bus this season, leading Tom to joke that television options on the road are better than what he gets at home. Although he isn't a practical joker, Tom always has a witty comment at the ready, something that comes through in his broadcasts. "He's just always got lines, always got something to say," said his wife, Judy.

That words come swiftly to Tom is good, because his job is all about talking. As a broadcaster he falls in a weird category: he is not officially a member of the team, but he does everything they do, from traveling on the bus to signing baseball cards. This year Tom got his own card, and while he is careful to remind autograph seekers that he is not a player, he seems to really enjoy the recognition, said Judy. "I think this just made him really feel like he was part of the team, even though he doesn't play," she said.

And like other members of the team he has resigned himself, and Judy, to a life of motion. Before Bowling Green the couple lived in Portland, Maine. Judy loved the state, but she knew they would have to leave, and when that time came she made a deal with her husband. They could get the dog he wanted so badly if she could name it something that reminded her of Maine. So when they moved to Kentucky they adopted a small dachshund mutt, and Judy named the little guy Moose.

Of course, the dog Tom wanted so badly is now her constant companion during the baseball season when Tom is rarely home.

She takes the dog around the area, seeing what Tom seldom has time to enjoy. When her husband first said he wanted to take a job in Bowling Green, Judy was apprehensive. Like many New Yorkers, she thought the Northeast of the country was the best place to live and couldn't imagine living anywhere else, especially in the middle of the country. But the moves required by Tom's job have forced her to broaden her horizons. And it has been fun, especially in Kentucky, where her education has included attending the Kentucky Derby.

Tom's is more limited to baseball. At least this year he has an office at the ballpark. Last year at this time the front-office staff didn't have offices, and the ballpark didn't have a parking lot. Now they have both, and attendance numbers that promise to climb as they enter the height of summer, and the promotions that accompany it.

Because the Hot Rod staff sold five-year season-ticket deals before they even opened the park, they are in a comfortable position. Now they just have to add to their revenue by using promotions to reel in even more people. Promotions like a Cave Shrimp bobble-head giveaway, whose tail, Tom proudly declares, bobbles. T-shirts and other freebies are all in the works for the coming weeks. Tonight's big deal is Friday-night fireworks and Axel the mascot's birthday. Axel, it turns out, is of unknown age, but this is the second birthday celebration the Hot Rods have held for him.

In the press box they provide their own entertainment, sometimes unintended. On one wall is a handwritten note addressed to Hank the broadcaster: "Dear Hank, you are easy on the eyes too. XXX A. K." In talking about a player one night while broadcasting over the radio, Hank described him as being of Greek and Cuban heritage. "I said, 'Women would find he's easy on the eyes,' and that's just one of those, quit when you're ahead, or in my case, behind," says Hank.

On the field the players are having their own fun. Because they arrived early this morning after a long bus ride and road trip, they didn't have to show up for batting practice. Instead, they made their way to the clubhouse and the field later in the afternoon to stretch and toss the ball around. A few also seem to have decided to play Frisbee.

The team racked up far more losses than wins in the Midwest League in which they play in April. At one point in late April they had nine losses in a row. May was better, with slightly more wins than losses. This month they seem to have finally hit their stride, and it is fast. They are close to leading the league in stolen bases, Tom explains as he arranges cords and other equipment for tonight's radio broadcast. He covers both his media and his broadcast jobs in one swoop, setting up for his broadcast while creating and advancing a reputation for the team the media will pick up and promote.

For the players any team in the Minors has the atmosphere of a start-up. They are as energetic and bold as the front-office staff, not because they want to make sure the Hot Rods are a success, but because they want to launch themselves out of the Minors. Chris Murrill is a perfect example.

Chris isn't taking any part in the goofing around. With a bat firmly gripped in his right hand he sits sideways on a picnic bench in the stands staring at the field. He has the well-defined body of an athlete and a not unhandsome face, but he gives off a vibe of almost angry impatience. He is out to prove himself, and as a thirty-fifth-round draft pick he knows he is going to have to work harder at proving himself than those drafted in earlier rounds. It is no different from any other business transaction:

the Rays invested less in Chris than those drafted higher, so they don't expect as much of a return. To get their attention he has to outshine the others. "You always have to prove yourself every day," he says. "Make them know and understand why you're here." It's something the twenty-one-year-old Alabama outfielder has had to do his whole life, in high school, junior college, and now in the Minors. He doesn't mind too much. It's what he's always wanted to do, and he's doing it. Just like his dad did before him.

Growing up in Mobile, Chris was surrounded by mementos from his father's glory days. Billy Murrill played football, basketball, and baseball and had a collection of newspaper articles, sports equipment, and other memorabilia from his playing days. He went the furthest in baseball, even playing professionally briefly before blowing out his knee. As a child Chris used to love looking at his father's contract and awards. "And I was like, 'Man, I want to do that,'" he says. There is a home video of Chris as a toddler already swinging a Wiffle bat. His older brother played baseball and pitched in college, but never made it further. His older sister played softball, but gave it up after high school.

Chris is taking things to another level. It is his second year in professional baseball, his first in full season. In Rookie ball last season his batting average was .306, and when his dad came to visit him a few weeks ago, he hit a home run. Next week Chris and two other Hot Rod players will play in the Midwest League All-Star Game, and Chris is pretty happy to be one of them. He is eager to advance, and this season things might just work out in his favor.

This time next year he hopes to be far away playing in AA, for the Rays' affiliate in Alabama, not far from where he grew up. Back home most of his friends have graduated from college and are in what Chris calls "the real world." It is a place he can avoid so long as he keeps playing baseball. "Because when you get paid to do something you love, you can't really beat that, especially playing a game," he says.

Jairo De La Rosa isn't in as much of a hurry, which is good, because this isn't his first time playing at this level. Jairo is tall, laid back, and friendly. Three years ago he was playing Class-A ball as a shortstop. Then the Rays approached him about converting to a pitching position. He agreed. He didn't have much of a choice. The Rays didn't want him as a shortstop, but they were willing to look at him as a pitcher. So he went back down the ladder he had worked so hard to climb. His journey began with his arrival in the United States from his native Dominican Republic in 2004. He was eighteen and spoke no English. Now he is twenty-four, pretty much fluent, and a husband and father. His upward climb was faster the second time. He started last season in Rookie ball and was up here in Bowling Green a week before the season ended.

But just because it was faster doesn't mean it was easier. Jairo has been out with a shoulder injury for a few days. It's something that has been bothering him since the beginning of the season, but until last week, when it got so painful he could no longer pitch, he didn't say anything. "Sometimes you just got to pitch," he explains. "I been converted as a pitcher now. I can't waste time."

Unfortunately, a lot of time will be wasted this season. His 8.88 ERA is not too impressive. If his shoulder doesn't improve in a few days, he'll have it checked again. He tries not to worry. After all, he says, "This is baseball, people get hurt, people never get hurt sometimes . . . But at least I'm not gonna be the last or not the first hurt," he says.

He also isn't the first in the family to chase the baseball dream. His older brother, Tomas, played in the bigs. Jairo watched his brother make it in professional baseball. Then he used his own experience playing in the field behind his house to do the same. In 2004 his brother got to see Jairo play in spring training.

Now they hardly even talk. The last time Tomas played in the United States was for the San Francisco Giants in 2006. For the past three years he has been playing in Japan, and the time difference makes it hard to coordinate conversations. The season is also longer, with Tomas spending ten months in Japan and only two back in the Dominican Republic.

Jairo spends half his time in the United States and the other half back home in the Dominican Republic with his wife and little girl. He has a visa for the season but is not able to bring his family along. In the Majors he thinks it may be easier, which is just "another inspiration" for him to get there. In the meantime, he keeps in touch with them through free video calls on the computer. It's hard on a relationship and something he warned his wife, Bethania Paredes, about before they married in October 2007. But, he says, "she supports me, tells me I have to work hard, which I like." She never complains about feeling lonely, and when he worries about leaving her he remembers his brother's advice—focus on baseball because that is what is best for you and your family. It is what pays the bills, both for the apartment Jairo shares with other players in Kentucky and for the home his wife and daughter occupy back in the Dominican Republic. Plus the shopping he likes to do at Macy's, Marshalls, and Payless Shoes. Sometimes he buys things for his wife and daughter, but, he admits with a slightly embarrassed grin, he often just shops for himself.

Last time he returned home his daughter cried when he tried to hold her. He had been gone six months, and the baby he left was now a one-year-old. She didn't remember him, but a few days later, he says, "I was her favorite person." As she gets older he knows the absences will be even harder. Promises of toys and ice cream upon his return won't always cut it. Even now he may have trouble keeping up. It is only June, and he has already promised her three ice cream cones.

On the field before the game the mascots celebrate a birthday Jairo's daughter would no doubt enjoy. It is full-blown mascot mania, with a penguin in red boots, a big red blob, a dog, a raccoon, a milk bottle, a tomato, and Wendy from Wendy's, all moving their bulky frames to dance music as part of a dance-off in honor of Axel's birthday. Every once in a while an announcer boots a mascot from the competition. Wendy makes an early exit for chit-chatting with Rosco, the team's monkey mascot. Rosco is next to go for reasons unknown other than being more annoying than your average mascot. Finally, only Axel and one or two others are left. The fans voice their vote for Axel with cheers.

After a little more monkeying around, with Rosco doing a lot of the monkeying, the odd costumed characters leave the field to the Hot Rods and the West Michigan Whitecaps of Comstock Park, Michigan. But before the professional players can throw their first pitch, at least two dozen amateurs offer their own first pitches. There are tiny boys who have to hop, a girl who tosses the ball underhand, and an older man who throws it pretty much straight down. In the stands fans go to "the Garage" for a drink and "the Body Shop" for souvenirs. And then, when the fans are busy eating and chatting, the real playing begins.

At the bottom of the first Chris lines out to the Whitecaps' second baseman. An inning or two later a Michigan batter is hit by a pitch. The player walks to first slowly and stands there while a trainer looks him over. The next batter hits it out of the park, and the batter trots home easily.

Eligio "Eli" Sonoqui watches it all from the Hot Rods' dugout. He is a big, soft-looking twenty-two-year-old who is as talkative and open as his teammate Chris Murrill is leery and guarded. He is also following in his father's footsteps, the same way Chris did. For Eli, though, things will end up a lot differently this season. They are already different, because for him following his father doesn't mean just picking up a bat; it also means roping bulls.

Although he was raised in Arizona, Eli spent his summers helping out on the family ranch in Sonora, Mexico, where his father, Eligio Sr., was raised. His namesake was a pitcher who played in Mexico and, according to Eli, even had an offer to play in the United States, but turned it down because he didn't want to leave his family. He ended up leaving them shortly after when he went to work in construction in Arizona. As he worked his way up from a day laborer to owning part of a construction company, Eligio Sr. continued to play baseball recreationally, and that is how Eli, the oldest of his three sons, learned to play. "When he would go play in stadiums, I would go play catch with him," says Eli.

Even today, as a first baseman for the Hot Rods, Eli still returns to the things his father taught him. His season hasn't been great so far. In April he batted .227 with six runs batted in and just one home run and one stolen base in the fifteen games he played. In May he had four runs batted in and no home runs or stolen bases, batting .250 in the nine games he played. But he remains optimistic and continues to fall back on his father's words. Recently, he was reminded of something his father said about having rhythm. "Because in baseball everything has to do with rhythm, having the same movement, and that's going to help you out in the long run," says Eli.

He learned about cattle ranching from his summers in Mexico.

The family also has a smaller ranch in Arizona where they do team roping, which involves a pair of riders lassoing the front of a steer and its hind legs as fast as they can. Eli competed in a few tournaments but never won anything.

In baseball he has had more success. He was drafted by the Tampa Bay Rays out of high school in the ninth round in 2006. He turned down three college offers to join the Rays, starting his career in professional baseball, a goal his family had set for him when he was young. "To realize I had the opportunity to play professional baseball," says Eli. "I took it for full advantage. Thankfully, I [am] here today, still playing."

The adjustment was difficult. In professional baseball, even at the low levels where he started, the pitching was better and so were the players. In high school Eli was one of the best; in professional ball, he says, everyone was "the best of the best."

But the higher level of play was not all that he had to get used to; he also had to learn how to live away from his family, something he had never done. To say Eli is close to his family is more than an understatement. Tattooed in large cursive letters on the bottom of his forearms are a *P* and a *G*, his grandfather's initials. When he goes home he talks of visiting not just his living relatives, but his deceased ones as well in the cemetery where they are buried.

It is from his family that he learned all he knows, baseball from his father, ranching from his grandfather, and car mechanics from his uncles. In Arizona his cousins have a body shop where he works whenever he can, building old cars, racing cars, and classic cars.

He does that in the off-season. During the season he focuses on baseball. His first season he learned how to hit the ball more consistently and how to be more aware of the situations that happen during a ball game. Between his first and second years of professional baseball he made a point of getting in better shape so that when he came back his second season he was faster on the field. Most important, though, he says, he worked on the mental aspect of the game. "Because you have to be ready before a pitch, before the game . . . have to be mentally ready from first pitch of game to last pitch."

And this year the number of games has increased for Eli. Before this season he had never played a full regular season, only the shorter season common in the game's lower rungs. Now that his season will include 140 games, the approaching three-day All-Star break is sounding pretty nice. He is planning to use it to go home to Arizona for his girlfriend's birthday, the first time he has been able to share it with her in the three years they have been dating. He plans to catch a plane home after Sunday's afternoon game and hopefully surprise her before she goes to bed.

When he returns to Bowling Green a few days later he will visit the National Corvette Museum if there is time. His talent with tools extends beyond the garage, and on the team he is known as "Handyman" and called frequently when other players need help fixing their air-conditioning.

The only thing he can't seem to fix is a strained rotator cuff in his right shoulder. In all his years as a cowboy he has never hurt himself, despite facing huge risks like getting your foot stuck in the stirrup or falling off your horse and being trampled. But in baseball he has broken a bone in his right hand and now has been out three weeks for his shoulder injury. He watches his team lose the game from the dugout and hopes in a week he will be back out there to help them win. His goal is to keep playing as long as he can. "If I can play the rest of my life, I would do it," he says. "If I have to use a cane to run or hold myself up, I would do it."

But the Minors are an industry, and a team can carry an injured player who has had a less than stellar season only so long. Eli is green enough to think a good attitude and hard work will take him as far as he wants to go. The season will teach him otherwise.

12. The Businessmen

Let's step back from the field for a bit and look at the people dressed not in uniforms, but in suits. Unlike in Lexington, where a single man is pretty much credited with bringing professional baseball to town, in Bowling Green the list is longer. Two of the more colorful characters credited with scripting the Hot Rods' story are a restaurateur and a politician.

The dining boss, Rick Kelley, also happens to be a Little League coach. Just a few miles from Bowling Green Ballpark where the Hot Rods play is a recreational ball field. Rick stands at home plate, hitting balls into the outfield for a group of nine- and ten-year-old boys. It is hot and sticky and creeping toward dark, but Rick keeps the boys running by calling out, "Take charge" and "Charge it" and "Let's go" as he hits balls their way. When a boy fails to call for a ball he is in the process of catching, Rick reprimands him, "That's your ball. Call for it." For a while afterward the boys call out loudly and emphatically every time a ball comes near them. Then they ease off and forget until Rick calls out once more, "Call for it." It is an hour into a two-hour evening practice, and the front of Rick's T-shirt is soaked in sweat. He tells the boys to take a break and studies a clipboard while his players head to the dugout for water.

The regular Little League season is over. These are the All Stars of their age group. They were chosen by their teammates based on talent, to play a series against two other teams, which will send the top two teams on to the district level. Rick took a group of eleven- and twelve-year-olds past district and state and all the way to regionals two years ago. They were the number-one seed going in but ended up losing 3–0 in the semifinals.

Rick isn't sure how this team will do when they compete next Friday and Saturday. A few seem less enthusiastic and tend to watch the ball hit the ground before making a move. But huddled together during their break they all talk excitedly about players likely to make next year's twenty-five-man active roster on their favorite Major League teams. The twenty-five-man roster is an elite class of an elite group, and one these boys will probably never know. Even if they are lucky enough to be drafted, they have only a 5 percent to 10 percent chance of making it to the Majors.[1]

And that is if they make it to professional baseball. Right now they haven't even made it to high school. Rick's baseball career ended right here, in Little League. A lot of men say they never made it past Little League, but most don't mean it quite like Rick does. He really never made it past Little League; he is fifty-five and has been coaching the same team in the nine- to twelve-year-old Little League Baseball Division, or Major Division, for more than three decades. It is an inordinately long time in a division where parent coaches often last about as long as their sons or daughters are eligible to play, that is, four years. Rick's oldest son is twenty-five, his daughter is twenty-four, and his middle son twenty. His youngest is eight and in all likelihood will be on Rick's team next year. "So I'll at least hang around until he's twelve," Rick says. After that he says he'll retire from coaching, at which point he may actually get to use his Hot Rod season tickets. After all he did to help bring the team to town, he might as well enjoy them.

And he has been, in a sense. His restaurant, Mariah's, located just a block or two from the ballpark, has seen customers come in for drinks before games and for food after games. The downtown stadium and team are achieving what Rick had hoped the Hot Rods would, drawing people back downtown to eat instead of heading to the outlying drag of chain restaurants. And that is exactly why Rick wanted a Minor League Baseball team in town. Rick may be a Little League coach, but first he is a businessman, a downtown businessman to be exact, same as much of his family. And as far back as he can count, at least four generations, that family has been in Bowling Green.

He joined the family office-supply business after graduating from Bowling Green's Western Kentucky University. A few years later, in 1980, about the same time he started coaching Little League, Rick opened Mariah's with a friend. He hadn't intended to make a career of the restaurant business. But that is what he has done. In 2005 he opened Buckhead Cafe, a fast-casual eatery about five miles from Mariah's. In November 2009 he opened the more upscale YOLOS Restaurant and Bar—You Only Live Once, Shuga—in Nashville with two of his children. But Mariah's, in the heart of downtown Bowling Green, remains his flagship. Situated in a huge brick house built in the early 1800s, it serves everything from the Kentucky classic and cholesterol-heavy hot brown—cheese, brown sugar, and bacon—to the lighter southwestern mahi tacos. On the walls are large murals that paint a picture of a downtown Bowling Green of yore when the city center, and not the urban sprawl that grew up around it, was the destination.

Rick has always been interested in making sure downtown Bowling Green thrives and is active and vibrant. When the city was talking downtown development earlier last decade and ideas came up that Rick didn't think would bring life back into the sagging downtown—like an assisted-living facility next to Mariah's—he started down the baseball path. It was a long road, and one he did not travel alone.

Mike Buchanon was right there with him. There were others, but as Warren County judge executive, the highest elected official in the county, Mike played a large part in getting baseball here. Like Rick, Mike's playing days ended with Little League. But as a fan he has carried his love of the sport to another level. When his children were young he used to take them to nearby Nashville and Louisville to see professional baseball games. He took it even further, literally, by using appointments with his allergist in Kansas City, Missouri, as an excuse to watch the Kansas City Royals play. How he ended up with an allergist more than five hundred miles away is a bit of a mystery considering he was born just eighteen miles from downtown Bowling Green and has lived in the city since he was seven. But that, I am afraid, is another story entirely.

Mike has been making a living in the real estate rental business since the early 1970s. He is a few years older than Rick and was roommates with Rick's older brother in college. His children, now grown, were coached by Rick when they played Little League.

Mike's quest to bring professional baseball to Bowling Green has lasted almost as long as Rick's Little League coaching career. But not quite — it began just a year or two after Mike took office as judge executive in 1993. "I liked the idea from the get-go," says Mike, who has a head full of curly gray hair and a dimple in his left cheek. "It brings people together, it brings people to a destination seventy nights out of the year, it stimulates business in downtown Bowling Green, and it creates excitement in the community." He could go on—and does. It helps convince businesses looking to relocate to the area that there is more to Bowling Green than what Mike describes as a good labor pool and good schools. There is also entertainment, something he feels the city has, in the past, been found to be lacking.

The Bowling Green Barons of the Kentucky-Illinois-Tennessee (or KITTY) League played in town from 1939 to 1942, but other than that, professional baseball doesn't seem to have left much of a mark on the city.[2] Mike wanted to change that, so in the mid-1990s he partnered with Johnny Webb, who was mayor at the time, to form a committee to study the idea of bringing professional baseball to the city. The results were disappointing. After talking to several different people, including local attorney Mike Reynolds, who had experience in the matter and is now a state senator, they determined it would be too expensive. And that was the end of Buchanon's first attempt to bring professional baseball to Bowling Green.

The second attempt came in 2003 and 2004 at the initiation of Rick and several other interested parties. That was after the city did some downtown development planning that Rick found wanting. After talking with Mike Reynolds, Rick also became convinced that baseball might be the way to go and, along with Mike Buchanon and several others, reached out to potential

Minor League Baseball owners. The result was Play Ball '05, an organizing committee devoted to studying the feasibility of Minor League Baseball in Bowling Green at a new ballpark. To make it all happen by 2005 they set out to sell two thousand season tickets by June 1, 2004, thereby proving the community's support to potential new owners and ensuring debt repayment. They ended up selling around fourteen hundred season tickets on a five-year commitment, says Rick. But the owner they were talking to didn't work out.

Mike Buchanon adds more color to the story. "Every team wants you to build them a ballpark. That's pretty much a given," says the judge executive. "But some of them also want cash infusions. And really, people ask for just about anything."

Either way you say it, the result was the same: they couldn't bring a Minor League team to Bowling Green or get a baseball field built in the city. That is, until the middle of the last decade when a tax-increment financing district was approved. After a certain amount of improvements are made, the TIF district allows a percentage of future increases in tax revenues within a downtown redevelopment area to go toward debt repayment. The ballpark became a cornerstone of the redevelopment effort.

But that was just how the stadium got built. They still needed a team. Art Solomon had one and was interested in buying another. The earlier work Play Ball '05 did to show community support for baseball went a long way toward convincing Solomon that buying the Columbus Catfish in Columbus, Georgia, and bringing them to Bowling Green was a good idea.

Mike didn't need any convincing to buy season tickets. He has a seat in the front row behind home plate and stopped by the park after work regularly the first season. Some nights he stayed only a few innings, but during that time he would walk the main concourse and see people he went to school with; people he knew from nearby Tennessee; people from Kentucky's capital, Frankfort; and even people from the state's largest city, Louisville.

Before the start of the second season he got his hands dirty inspecting the ivy planted on the stadium's exterior walls. He just can't seem to get enough of a sport that is about community and family and "all the things that we appreciate about life," he says.

For Mike, those things would not include Cave Shrimp, a name proposed for the team that Mike detested. His opposition was so well known that the team decided to play a trick on him before their first season. At the time Rick Kelley worked right next door to the team's front office and was in on the joke. He called Mike and told him the front office wanted to tell him the team's name before announcing it to everyone else. When Mike arrived Rick took him back to general manager Brad Taylor, who presented the judge executive with a Cave Shrimp T-shirt and told him that is what the team was going to be called. "You could just see him boiling underneath, but he tried to be a good sport about it," says Rick, chuckling at the memory. They let him know it was a joke a few minutes later and went on to use the same idea for their "What Could've Been Night" promotion that proved so successful that first year.

Back at the Little League field this season, the sky has gone from a deep blue to a darker shade of blue-black, and mosquitoes are biting. A group of boys on another team who look no older than four or five has finished their practice and are chasing each other around the bleachers. Their older cohorts continue to field balls that Kelley hits without pause. The boys are tiring, and the only sound is the cicadas, the slap of the bat, and Kelley's voice—"Go get it . . . Great hustle, Clay . . . Can't stand there and watch"—trailing after them as they run for balls.

13. Kings of the Road

Not being allowed on the team bus, I drive my own car and meet up with the team during one of their series in Fort Wayne, Indiana. Much of the team's time is spent on the road, and while most of the front-office staff stays behind, that doesn't mean business is left behind. Everything is orchestrated, and access to the players is no easier away from Bowling Green than it is in Bowling Green.

When not on the bus, at the ballpark, or eating, the players tend to stay in their rooms and rest. I didn't want to knock on their hotel room doors. Maybe if I was the stereotypical sportswriter, overweight, older, and, most important, male, it would have worked. But as a relatively young, single woman, it just didn't seem right.

So I go grocery shopping—with team trainer Scott Thurston. Away from Bowling Green Scott ends up taking on a lot of the more mundane tasks of fielding a baseball team, like debating whether to purchase smoked or regular turkey. Important stuff, but then, when it gets down to it, the everyday business of baseball can be downright boring.

The biggest challenge Scott faces at present is figuring out how to purchase pregame snacks for the Hot Rod players and coaches, about thirty-five people, on exactly $40 a day at a Meijer supermarket. The players will eat anything, he explains, which is good, because on that kind of budget you can't buy a lot of meat. Peanut butter and jelly are more like it. The food isn't supposed to be a meal, but for a lot of the players that's what it is. Either they oversleep and don't have time to go get food before the game, or they don't buy much at lunch because they don't want to burn through their limited meal-money funds, usually about $20 a day. So Scott tries to buy items that provide a lot of energy. As the team's trainer he is the closest thing they have to a dietitian.

He has just snagged five bags of apples and four of oranges when Tom Gauthier, the team's broadcaster, appears with two bags of chips and three salsas, wanting to know if that will be enough. It will, says Scott for one day. It's the first day of their four day series in Fort Wayne, and they don't plan on coming back to Meijer, so they are loading up. Jared Elliott, who handles strength and conditioning, shows up with a dozen loaves of bread. Shopping for the team's pregame snack isn't really in any of their job descriptions. But at this level, if it doesn't involve a bat or a ball, it usually falls into the hands of Jared or Scott. Tom comes along to help out. "I'm basically the mother of the family," says Scott.

He is their first line of medical assistance for injuries—and the one who buys them vanilla wafers. If he buys more food than the players eat, he brings the leftovers back to Bowling Green and gives them to the clubhouse manager, who is in charge of the pregame snack for home games but does not travel with the team. If Scott spends more than he was allotted, then he has less to spend on the next road trip. This time he has about $600 to cover groceries, trips to the gym, medical supplies, taxis, and anything else that might come up during the series. After unloading sixteen loaves of bread, almost a dozen bags of fruit, countless bags of chips, and huge containers of salsa, peanut butter, and mayonnaise onto the checkout counter, Scott stands back and watches the register tally his items. The cashier wants to know if he is having a party. I wish, he says.

Sometimes he offers more of an explanation. Today he just lets it go. It fits his cool-cat image. It is eighty degrees outside, but he is wearing long pants, a dark Tampa Bay Rays Windbreaker, and a newsboy cap. He is just a little thinner, paler, and quieter than the athletes he works with. At thirty-one he is also older. He first went to college to play baseball and did that for a couple of years before realizing education offered him a better future. Being an athletic trainer was a way to stay in sports. Working in baseball was the logical next step for him, a former baseball player. He has been with the Tampa Bay Rays since 2008.

His first year with them he was in Princeton, West Virginia—"That was a fun one"—followed by a season in Fishkill, New York. Compared to those places, Bowling Green is a step up. It isn't Greeley, Colorado, where he lives in the off-season, but then there isn't much time during the season to do the hiking and other outdoor activities he enjoys in his home state.

The groceries come to $147.05, and he pays in cash, careful to pocket the receipt for bookkeeping reasons. Outside they load the groceries into the luggage area underneath the team bus. The food will remain there until they get to the field later this afternoon and it can be taken into the clubhouse. As they step onto the bus themselves, the trio debates what they want to eat for lunch. Scott is in the mood for Thai. Tom nixes that with a shake of his head, Jared with the remark that he just had Chinese. They settle on Cracker Barrel, a trademark of life on the road in this part of the country. It is early August, and they have already been to Fort Wayne three times this season and sampled all the nearby restaurants. By now "nothing ever sounds good anymore," says Tom.

This season his wife, Judy, accompanied him on the road only twice, once to Lansing, Michigan, and once to a town somewhere in Wisconsin whose name she can't remember. "Some of these towns you don't really want to visit again," she said. The year before, when the Hot Rods were in a different league and touring the more appealing cities of Savannah, Asheville, and Charleston, she joined Tom on the road more often. It's a way to see him during the season.

Judy opted not to come to Fort Wayne, and Tom would probably have as well if he had a choice. The Quality Inn where they are staying is in the outskirts of the city, a place with a lot of big-box shops and few sidewalks and crosswalks. At the restaurant they immediately launch into a discussion about postgame meals. At this level players get nothing after the game, but the staff is served a meal by the home team. The Fort Wayne TinCaps happen to put together a pretty good spread. Not as good as some places.

Tom talks about one place where there were multiple options and a woman who basically took his order. He pulls out a Hot Rod pocket schedule to try to remember when they were there. By this time in the season the trips tend to run together, and so do the days. Until someone told Tom what day it was earlier, he had forgotten today was Saturday. Scott can't remember the ballpark Tom is talking about, and the conversation fizzles out while they eat.

Then Tom brings up "Dirty," one of Scott's two alter-ego drinking personas. "Stu" is the other, a happy, smart-ass drunk. Dirty is the crazy, almost-pass-out drunk who does things like lick elbows. Dirty has made only one appearance this year, and Tom wants to know if he will be making another tonight. After games in Bowling Green they head to the few places that are open late, Overtime Sports Bar & Grill, Double Dogs, and Utleys Bar & Grill. On rare days off Tom, his wife, and Scott hang out at the pool at the apartment complex where they all live.

On the road there is a curfew. An hour and a half after the bus returns to the hotel from the ballpark, players are supposed to be in their rooms. Some managers check rooms. Hot Rod field manager Brady Williams doesn't, unless someone gets in trouble. It doesn't seem likely that Dirty will make an appearance tonight. Their six-hour bus ride began at six this morning, and they are dragging a bit. With a late game last night there wasn't much time to sleep, and by the time they are done with lunch today there won't be time to nap. As they wait for Scott to finish his meal, Jared tries his luck at a wood puzzle on the table. If Scott is the countercultural skater type, Jared is the classic old-school athlete, with short blond hair, a dark tan, chiseled bones, and huge biceps.

He got into strength and conditioning after he blew out both knees playing football and basketball in high school. He is twenty-six and spent last off-season waiting tables in New York City. Like Scott he is from Colorado, and because of their backgrounds and jobs they end up spending a lot of time together on the road. They joke that they're like a common-law married couple. They head back to the same hotel together after a night of drinking and leave the same hotel together to go out to eat the next morning. It's kind of like what they talked about last night, how there are a lot of things they do in baseball that might seem unusual outside of the sport.

In baseball, says Tom, "the general rules of life don't apply." Not that there isn't structure. There is plenty of that, and all three of them are a part of that vast system, trying to work their way up to the top. For Scott right now there is a "logjam" of trainers in the Rays organization, so his chances of moving up next year are not great. He is on a one-year contract; Jared signs for the season. Both expect to renew. Tom is a little more of his own entity. He doesn't work his way up in an organization so much as look for higher-up broadcasting jobs in whatever organiza-tion he can find them. Like with the players, it will take not just talent but luck as well for Tom to move up. If he didn't have the talent, his wife said she would encourage him to do something else. "Because there are other careers where I could see him a lot more, or he'd be making a lot more money," said Judy. "But this is something he wants to do, and he's good at it."

Of course, he has had slipups. Since becoming a professional baseball broadcaster Tom has never sworn on air, but it has hap-pened to him. It was back in his college days when he thought he had turned the mike off and hadn't. With the Hot Rods he hasn't had any real major screwups, although last home stand he called a home run, and then the ball hit only halfway up the wall and went right into the glove of the opposing team. It was pretty bad, he admits. "I said, 'That ball's gone. Oh, no, it hit the top of the wall.' It wasn't even close to being gone," he says. "I don't know how I butchered it so bad." Sometimes you can recover, but that error was pretty blatant. All he could do was tell the listeners he had screwed up. His broadcasts can be heard live on a local radio station back in Bowling Green and over the

Internet. His wife's friends like to joke they can also be heard on the phone. "His voice is normally an announcer voice. My friends make fun of him," said Judy.

After lunch the trio heads back to the hotel for an hour or so of rest before taking the bus to the ballpark. At the ballpark Tom heads to the press area and pages through a binder filled with league and team standings and other figures he may need to add to his broadcast. In a separate box he keeps cards on which are written fun tidbits, little baseball quotes or facts he has read or overheard and likes to drop in when he can. Right after the game he writes a game story for the Hot Rod website in a half hour, a necessity developed last season when the bus left for the hotel almost exactly forty-five minutes after the game ended.

When all the work is done and the bus has taken them back to the hotel, he likes to get a drink with manager Brady Williams and the other coaches and listen to their old baseball stories. Of course, they don't always talk about baseball. Last time they talked about eyebrow waxing. Tom doesn't elaborate. He knows Brady's father, Jimy, a former big league manager with Toronto, Boston, and Houston, listens to his radio broadcasts, which adds a little more pressure to his job. "So I can't say anything and have the average baseball fan believe," says Tom. "I have to know what I'm talking about." It's true. It might not happen every night, but most nights Brady says his father listens to the game on the radio so they can talk about it afterward.

Brady is standing near the visiting team's dugout, watching his players take batting practice. Parkview Field is new and big and right downtown. It is the kind of place that attracts large crowds and is already sold out for tonight's Saturday-night game. There are teams with fields that are little more than glorified high school ballparks. This isn't one of them.

Brady has seen a lot of fields in his days. As a child he saw the Major League fields where his father worked. In his own playing days he spent five years in the Minor Leagues, making it up to AA and then two years in independent baseball. This is his first year with Bowling Green, his fifth in coaching. He is thirty. And he still gets advice from his dad. It doesn't motivate Brady so much as keep him on an even keel, keep him from getting too high or too low. "It's easy to fall into the wave of going up and down, and you got to try to stay the same as much as you can," he says.

His father helps him with that, and he in turn does the same for his players. At this level one of the most important things they have to learn is to be professional, to come to the park every day and be the same player regardless of how well or badly they performed the day before. That is what is going to take them further; that is what Brady tries to instill in them and what he tries to practice himself.

In that respect, managing and playing are similar, but in other ways they are very different. As a player your goal is to try to help yourself get better; as a manager you are trying to help others get better. And when Brady says that is why he likes managing, you tend to believe him.

There are difficult features of his job, like releasing a player or not being able to get through to a talented player. Sometimes what he needs them to understand has to do with what they do on the field; other times it is about how they act on the road or dress off the field. Whatever it is, Brady never stops trying to help. Because, he says, that's his job.

Then there is the business side of it. Brady has been around the game long enough and worked his way up far enough to understand it is a business. There is money involved, and just like in the stock market you want to try to get the most out of your investment, which can mean making sure a player with a huge signing bonus gets the playing time to ensure he fulfills his potential. But having been a player himself, Brady knows players are more than just investments and is careful when he talks about Eli Sonoqui, the injured infielder who grew up on a ranch and always has a minute for everyone. "I think Eli, in whatever he does, whether it's baseball or something else, he's gonna be good at it," says Brady. Eli enjoyed the game; he enjoyed getting better and did get better. What Brady doesn't say is that Eli apparently didn't get good enough. The Hot Rods released Eli on July 3, just in time for Independence Day. The first baseman never had a chance to play again after straining his rotator cuff in mid-May.

Reached back home in Arizona, Eli recounted his last days with the team. A few days before he was released he said his arm stopped hurting and he was able to hit baseballs in batting practice. He was feeling good and told team trainer Scott Thurston he was ready to play. But they wouldn't release him from the disabled list. The next few days were incredibly exasperating. Eli was ready to play, he wanted to play, but he was not allowed to play, and there was nothing he could do to change the situation. "I was frustrated and hurt," he said. "I didn't cry, but it was to the point that was what I feel [like doing]."

The last day of that home series he could tell when he looked at Brady that something was wrong. During the game each coach came by and talked to him, not just about baseball, but about life in general. After the game Eli stayed to watch the fireworks and sign autographs, knowing without being told that it might be his last chance to do so as a Hot Rod. When he finally made his way to the clubhouse, he was met with dead silence. Usually, there was music and chatter, this time nothing. Brady asked to see him in his office, and that is when Eli learned he was being released. "I took it hard. I was teary-eyed," he said. "I always dreamed of playing professional baseball, all my life. To say you released takes it right out of my hands."

After thanking Brady for the chance to play in the Rays organization, Eli told him he would be back playing baseball. This wouldn't be the last time they saw him. Then he went home to Arizona and enrolled in a yearlong course to become an automotive technician. The baseball chapter in his life wasn't done, he said. He just needed something to fall back on.

Chris Murrill went the opposite direction. The restless outfielder from Alabama was assigned to the Charlotte Stone Crabs Class-A (advanced) in Port Charlotte, Florida, the day after Eli was released. Brady describes Chris as a treat. During the seventy games Chris played for Bowling Green he batted .292, had two home runs, had twenty-two runs batted in, and stole twenty-eight bases. He wanted to get better so quickly, wanted to be the best he could be right now. He was one of those guys who doesn't understand it takes time, says Brady, that you can't become a big league player over night. But he did get better, says Brady, maybe ten times better than a year ago. And that is why he isn't with the Hot Rods anymore.

Jairo De La Rosa hasn't gone anywhere. The well-dressed pitcher from the Dominican Republic is still sidelined with an injured shoulder. But he is nevertheless wearing a uniform, says Brady. He is yet in the game. Brady worked with Jairo before when he was a position player and knows he has a good arm, and that is why the Rays decided to convert him to a pitcher. He also knows if Jairo didn't make the switch, his career might have ended. So while it was a hard transition to make, not making it wasn't really an option. Only now the Dominican pitcher isn't playing, and they haven't been able to figure out what is wrong with his shoulder. It's tough because a lot of things go through your mind, says Jairo. "I going to get a surgery or not. I going to come back and pitch or not," he says.

Injuries are not good for baseball players. They are especially bad for pitchers. When he originally converted to a pitcher more than a season ago, Jairo thought it was easy. Throw a few innings, get out, take a shower, and then return to the stands to watch the rest of the game. Now he believes it is one of the harder roles. "As a pitcher, all you have is your arm," he says. "If you're not 100 percent, you're not good."

There is nothing he can do. He tries to help the team in other ways. When Latin players are assigned to the Hot Rods, he is unofficially put in charge of showing them the ropes, making sure they are on time, taking them places they need to go, and otherwise trying to ease the adjustment. Today one of the American players called him "Dominican Dad." "At least that makes me feel better," says Jairo. "At least I'm doing something with my teammates."

During the games he sometimes videotapes the hitters so the coach can critique them later. Other times he communicates by walkie-talkie with the bullpen, letting them know when a relief pitcher needs to get ready to go into the game. He started that two nights ago and will continue until the Hot Rods lose. Then he will have to step down so someone with more luck can take over.

Off the field he tries to stay away from shops. Last time the team had a day off he jokingly asked another player to hold his wallet so he wouldn't be tempted to spend money. He doesn't have a lot to look forward to right now, except maybe being home in time for his birthday on September 8. He would like to go home now.

Instead, he sits in the dugout, a huge pack of ice strapped to his right shoulder with an elastic bandage. It is an hour or so before game time, and the last of his teammates are finishing up some exercises on the field with strength and conditioning coach Jared Elliott before heading into the clubhouse to get ready for the game.

Jairo has done everything he can do to get ready, but his arm isn't cooperating. Trainer Scott Thurston's goal is to get him playing for the last week of the season. But based on how he is feeling now, Jairo doesn't think that will happen. If the team makes the playoffs, and they have a chance of that, just about a game out of making them right now, he thinks he might be able to play then, but not before then and not tonight.

It is a nice night, and the stands are packed. Most of the action occurs in the last two innings, with the TinCaps winning the game 6–5. The loss means the Hot Rods are that much further from making the playoffs, and Jairo no longer has a job manning the walkie-talkies.

After the game Tom Gauthier, Jared Elliott, Scott Thurston, and some of the coaches grab a few beers, watch a mixed martial arts competition on television, and shoot some pool. They talk about the game, baseball rules, fantasy football, and punk music, among other things. Tom reports all of this back to me. Manager Brady Williams did not want me hanging out with them. At one point Tom even asks if I can leave out the part about them drinking beer. They are so worried about bad press, they risk appearing as dull as the most straightlaced accountants. Scott is probably as off the cuff as the Hot Rods get, and Tom's humor can be pretty entertaining. When Scott, the team's trainer, complained about not having a walkout song, Tom played him one—"King of Pain."

A month later their season ends with sixty-one wins and seventy-eight losses. They don't make it to the playoffs, and Jairo never plays again.

15. Bowling Green Hot Rods first baseman Eligio "Eli" Sonoqui. Joey Hayes Photography.

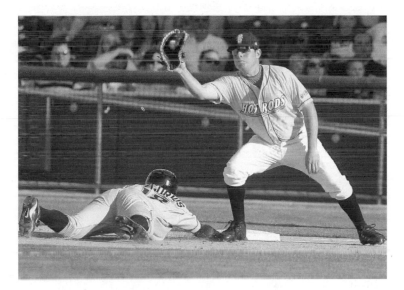

16. (*Opposite*) Bowling Green Hot
Rods outfielder Chris Murrill. Joey
Hayes Photography.

17. (*Above*) Bowling Green Hot
Rods first baseman Eligio "Eli"
Sonoqui. By Alex Slitz, *Daily News*.

18. (*Opposite top*) Bowling Green Hot Rods strength and conditioning coach Jared Elliott. By Alex Slitz, *Daily News*.

19. (*Opposite bottom*) Bowling Green Hot Rods broadcaster Tom Gauthier. By Alex Slitz, *Daily News*.

20. (*Above*) Bowling Green Hot Rods outfielder Chris Murrill talks with fans. By Alex Slitz, *Daily News*.

21. Bowling Green Hot Rods outfielder Ty Morrison is congratulated
by teammates after scoring a run. By
Alex Slitz, *Daily News*.

Part 4
Florence Freedom:
The Humble Life

14. Falling Down

There are the Majors, there are the Minors, and then there is independent baseball. When the Lexington, Louisville, and Bowling Green teams learned I would be including the independent Florence Freedom in my book, they scoffed. They didn't want to be grouped with Florence and relented only after making sure I understood Florence was nowhere near their level. They wanted a clear separation. It was easy for them: they were in the Minors.

It was harder for those in Florence, especially the ones who had been in the Minors. They wanted to believe the divide was not as large as their former teammates would like to think. The truth is the climb down is only slight, but the hike back up is steep. It is a journey few are willing to take. Any chance at fame and fortune seems impossibly far away. Down here humility is not the exception; it is the rule.

Toby Rumfield knows this better than most. His children

haven't quite caught on. His oldest, Sam, is twelve years old and knows Pete Rose. At least that's what she says. She also says she's been held by a lot of famous people. "My dad tells me sometimes when we go to Reds games, 'Man, that person over there held you when you were little.' I'm like, 'Whoa, that's cool.'" She rattles off a few of her more famous "holders"—Reba McEntire, a really famous and nice baseball player whose name she can't remember, and a bunch of famous mascots, like the hawk whose exact name she has also forgotten. "Didn't you get held by Mickey Mouse?" asks her nine-year-old brother, T. J. She did and by countless other Disney characters. That was back when her dad, Toby, was still playing professional baseball and they spent a lot of time in Florida for spring training, and thus at Walt Disney World. T. J., whose full name is Toby Joseph, adds that he has been held by Cincinnati Reds player Brandon Phillips and by Atlanta Braves player Larry Wayne "Chipper" Jones. They don't mention anyone famous having held Justin, their six-year-old brother. By the time he came along their father's playing days were pretty much over. Now Toby is teaching a five-year-old in a tie-dye T-shirt how to hit. The boy's father stands to the side, talking on his cell phone and offering pointers.

It is a cold and rainy January afternoon, and the temperature inside the old storage unit in which Toby is coaching is low enough to require gloves. An industrial heater blasts warm air at one end of the makeshift batting cage, but every time someone walks through the door at the other end, a cold draft enters. Sam sits at a tiny desk, plastic sheeting shielding her from her father and his students. On the back of the door to her left is a Florence Freedom poster with the message "Welcome to the baseball academy!!!" written in pen at the bottom.

The academy is a new thing, another way for Toby and a few

other players and staff to pull in a little extra cash. They put the whole thing together themselves, rolling turf onto the floor, arranging batting cages, and hanging tarp and plastic sheeting to separate the various areas and complete the look. Charging children thirty-five dollars a half hour for lessons is just one way to boost the thirty thousand dollars a year or so Toby gets as manager for the Florence Freedom.

Managing an unaffiliated team, a team that has no relationship with a Major League organization, a team where players aren't trying to get to the Majors so much as break into affiliated baseball, is not where he pictured he'd be at this point in his life. He was supposed to be across the river in Cincinnati, playing for the Reds, the team that selected him in the second round of the 1991 draft. He signed straight out of high school for what seemed like a promising bonus at the time—a little more than one hundred thousand dollars.

Twenty years later, the sweet deal has soured. Not only is he in unaffiliated ball, but he is with a team known more for scandal away from the ballpark than success in the stadium. As bad as it seems, by the end of the season things will actually be worse. His lesson in humility, it seems, has only just begun.

If he could do it over, he would have gone to college. Instead, he is almost forty and taking online courses. He started those recently, to set an example for his three children. "But you never know how it's going to end up," he says. "I mean, there's a lot of guys go on second round, five years later they're in big leagues making millions."

Toby wasn't one of them. At first it seemed like he might be. He spent about four years working his way through the lower levels of the Minor League system in West Virginia, Montana, and North Carolina. He moved steadily up from Rookie to

Class-A (low) and then Class-A (advanced) ball. His last year in Class-A he hit twenty-nine home runs and figured he was on the fast track to the bigs.

Then he spent four years in AA. He met the woman he would marry, Kari, his second year playing AA ball in Chattanooga, Tennessee. He wasn't looking to get married; he was a single ballplayer still on the rise, and he was having the time of his life. But there she was, managing the Outback Steakhouse where the players spent their Sunday nights. Six months later they were married with a baby on the way.

Then he was released. The Atlanta Braves picked him up, and he spent a year playing AA ball for them before finally breaking into AAA ball in 1999. Both that season and the next he played in Braves exhibition games, getting his first Major League hit off Dodgers pitcher Kevin Brown on March 29, 2000. But in the end he always got sent back down to AAA. He has a pretty good idea why he never lasted in the Majors. "I wasn't a top-of-the-line catcher, and I knew that. Maybe my flexibility in my hips or whatnot," he says. "But I could hit. I could always hit."

The only thing is, the catchers who made it to the bigs and stayed there were usually stronger defensively, he says. There just didn't seem to be room for a power-hitting catcher like Toby. But that didn't stop him from trying. In 2001 he played AAA ball for the Chicago White Sox. The following year he started with the Montreal Expos and then got traded to the Florida Marlins during spring training. It gets hard to follow after that. There are more trades and more time spent in AAA, always just one step away from the Majors.

In 2003, when the Houston Astros released him the last day of spring training, he knew his dream was coming to an end. He'd been playing Minor League Baseball for thirteen years and had never played in the Majors during the season. Still, baseball was what he did, and he wasn't ready to give it up yet. So he spent a year playing independent baseball. It was the first time since he was drafted out of high school that he was playing for a team that had no affiliation with a Major League team. And it was the best year he ever had in professional baseball. The team won the championship, and he felt he was a big part of that. He enjoyed independent baseball so much he took a job managing a team the following year. But he "still had it in his system," and halfway through the season, when the team's owner wouldn't let him recruit the players he wanted, he turned himself into a manager-player. "It didn't go over as well as I thought it would go over," he says. "After that I knew it was done."

He liked managing, but he had three children now, and the job didn't provide health insurance, so he took a job as a scout. He did that for two years before returning to managing. It's now been several years and several jobs since he played, but to fully let go, to know he's never, ever going to get to play in the Majors, is tough, and there are still days he thinks he could do it, that the dream is still possible. The only thing that gives him comfort is the knowledge that he did everything he could to get there.

He just wasn't good enough. Those are his words. And they are hard for him to utter. Even now, at thirty-seven, instructing a skinny kid how to load, balance, and leverage, he mentions people he still knows across the river in the Reds' front office. Dressed in baggy sweatpants, his red hair peeking from beneath a winter cap, he resembles a large outdoorsman more than a baseball player, but fans still recognize him. It helps that he is just fifteen minutes away from the team that drafted him. But that proximity is also a daily reminder of how close he got.

His wife, Kari, was just as close, and physically still is. She works in the Freedom front office as the team's general manager. "The first couple years I was married to Toby, I really thought he was going to be in the big leagues and I'd be the big league wife hanging out in the stands, supporting him, and raising our children," she says. She looks around her office, the huge white board covered in notes about the status of corporate sponsors, the sample toy promotional giveaway on her desk, the phone and computer. "That's not what happened," she says with a laugh.

Instead, she is the one making the bigger bucks, the one with the job that moved the family to Florence. Toby is with this team because of her first and because he is a great field manager second. It didn't start that way. In the beginning she was the one left behind, the one pulling the U-Haul with all their stuff to wherever they would spend the season while he flew ahead with the team on a private jet. That was when Toby was with the Braves and playing in the big league team's exhibition games. Later, when it was clear his chance at the bigs had passed, things got harder. The children were young, and getting released meant not having health benefits. That's around the time Kari started working again. At first it was just a way for her to pass the time and bring in a little extra money after their third child was born. The owner of the team Toby was with asked her to make some sales calls from home, and she started with a phone book and phone. She really didn't know her product. "I understood marketing outfield billboards, all that, but I really had no idea what I was selling," she says. "I was just calling people up, you know, introducing myself, building a relationship."

She has always been good at that. An attractive blonde, her North Dakota background and dimples lend her a wholesomeness that has served her well in sales, first in restaurant franchises and now in baseball. Within a month of her first baseball venture, the owner was paying her so much in commission he wanted to hire her full time. Four years later she had worked herself up to front-office general manager with another team. Word got around that she could sell, and in 2007 the owner of the Florence Freedom, Clint Brown, recruited her.

Toby followed two years later. Clint hadn't intended to hire Toby. Having a married couple on staff meant if he lost one, he lost both. But then by the time Toby came on board, his own wife and daughter were working for the team. "We've kind of embraced nepotism as a corporate strategy," he jokes.

His adult daughter, Deidra, manages food and beverage, and his wife, Kim, is the director of community relations. Kim has a background in banking and hails from this area. Clint is from nearby Indiana but lived in places like New York, San Francisco, and Phoenix before his work in market information brought him to northern Kentucky.

He is a big, balding man of fifty-five, with a round face, round belly, and expressive arms. Before owning a baseball team he owned his own business, Alliance Research, which measured and enhanced customer satisfaction. In plain English his company called customers on behalf of companies that had provided them a service and asked them to evaluate that service. Then he used what he found to counsel the companies on how to improve their services. Oh, and made a lot of money along the way.

By the time he sold his company in 1999, he says, it was one of the top of its kind in the business. He stayed on for three years and retired in 2002. He signed a three-year noncompete agreement and did what he had not been able to do for the past twenty-five years: he coached his children's sports teams, built a house, traveled for fun, and otherwise enjoyed himself. As one year slipped into two, the idea of returning to seventy hour workweeks, stomachaches, and constant business travel became harder and harder to imagine. Clint had watched some of his friends turn hobbies into second careers, and he thought he might try the same thing. So he made a list of the ideal circumstances for his new occupation, citing things like being a bigger part of the community, traveling less for work, and being a part of something his family could get involved in. "And who would know that this bankrupt, crappy little independent baseball team would meet every single one of my criteria," he says.

Around the same time Clint was looking for a new occupation, Florence Freedom came to town. Clint didn't pay much attention, hadn't even heard of the team that came to Florence and started playing in 2003, more than forty miles away in Hamilton, Ohio. Then, in 2004, the team went under, and news about it became hard to ignore. "Words like *bankruptcy* and *prison*, all those catch your attention," says Clint.

It was a pretty big story, and one the local populace has yet to forget. Shortly after Champion Window Field opened in Florence in the summer of 2004 contractors accused the team's ownership group, Northern Kentucky Professional Baseball, of not paying for work on the stadium and began filing liens against the group that totaled more than four million dollars by late August. In September Northern Kentucky Professional Baseball declared bankruptcy. In 2005 part owner Chuck Hildebrant was sentenced to five years in federal prison following a federal investigation over the financing of the around eight-million-dollar stadium.[1] It was a friend who suggested Clint rescue the team. "By this time, of course, this is like a four-letter word. Florence Freedom is synonymous with really evil things, and I'm thinking, 'You've gotta be crazy,'" he says.

But the more he thought about it, the more it made sense.

It not only met all his criteria, but would also be an easy act to follow. He knew nothing about running a baseball business, but he figured anything he did would be an improvement over bankruptcy. And that is how he came to own the team. It wasn't an easy purchase. There were actually a number of different outfits interested in buying the team, and they all had a plan. There were a lot of lawyers. Clint's background was checked, his fingerprints taken, his banker investigated.

Just about when he figured it wasn't going to happen, a bankruptcy judge approved his three-million-dollar purchase of the team. And that is when the fun started. With the help of the city he was able to offer creditors partial payments on the debts incurred by the previous ownership. Basically, everyone settled for fifty cents on the dollar, or costs, he says. But not everyone was happy, and to this day there are still hard feelings. "If I had been a little smarter, maybe I would have changed the name of Florence Freedom to something else," he says. "Because every once in a blue moon we still hear, 'Florence Freedom—you're the guys that screwed my partner.'"

But it wasn't Clint who screwed them. It was the previous owners, and he compares the accusations to blaming a new neighbor for stealing tools that the previous occupant took. There was no buyer's honeymoon for Clint. In Minor League and independent baseball the first year a team comes to town is usually a sort of honeymoon when everybody gets excited and wants to be a part of it. That's when people buy season tickets, sign on to sponsor, and organize group outings. Most teams have their best sales that first year and hold on tightly in the years that follow.

But Clint had nothing to hold on to. The team's first year had been played more than forty miles away, its second year embroiled in scandal. There had never been a honeymoon for the Freedom and no recapturing it. Instead, Clint had to re-earn the fans' trust, and it hasn't come cheap. He has yet to break even on the venture.

Surprisingly, having a Major League team just across the river isn't what has cost him. They're a competitor for attendance, but way down on the list, down past amusement parks, aquariums, and parish festivals. Yes, parish festivals. When "St. Joe" has a festival that attracts ten thousand people, that hurts the Freedom, says Clint. And in Florence there are plenty of parish festivals.

It may be just across the river from Ohio and the Midwest, but Florence has a southern charm all its own. Its water tower bears the words *Florence Y'all*. There is a story there and several others that add up to make the city of around twenty-eight thousand more than simply a suburb of Cincinnati.

The story of the team's name can be summed up by the period in which it was bought and moved to Florence not long after 9/11, when the country was still swimming in patriotism. The stadium was painted red, white, and blue. Clint did away with the red and blue, but kept the name. He had bigger concerns and figured even if he changed the name, the team would forever be known as the former Florence Freedom because of its notoriety. Plus, they had 99 percent name recognition, he jokes. Now he wishes he had changed it, but admits that after more than a half decade he still hasn't come up with a better name.

Those are the drawbacks. Otherwise, the endeavor is a fantasy come to life. For thirty years Clint has played fantasy baseball. He has been in one game since 1986. He is commissioner of a league and has a spreadsheet that "would knock your socks off." He likes to joke that owning the Freedom is kind of like a merger of fantasy baseball and Monopoly, except with real money. It is something he dreamed about as far back as the early 1990s, but never really thought would be a reality. And, at first, he didn't think an independent team counted. Like so many others he looked down on it, thought it wasn't the real thing.

He has learned otherwise. Watching some of the top-level teams in the Frontier League in which Florence plays, he knows it is just a question of luck, timing, and a few other factors that separate independent players from affiliated players. He has also come to appreciate the second chance that unaffiliated ball provides. "We're giving kids who have some talent and some ability, and they've stumbled along the way for one reason or another, and we're their second chance," he says. He loves that, and isn't so sure he would love the kind of players he thinks he would meet in the lower levels of affiliated ball. The kind of players who have never stumbled, have money in their pockets from signing bonuses, players who maybe aren't as humble, or as hungry to play as they are in unaffiliated ball.

In unaffiliated ball he tries to get to know his players, has them over to his house every year for a pig roast. He got to know Trevor Hall better than most. Trevor was a veteran player when Clint bought the team. He was great with kids, great with fans, and a star in the Frontier League in which he had played for some time. He had great numbers in 2005, including around twenty-three home runs. In 2006 he had one year left before he would be too old to play in the league, and he was expecting to have a great season.

You can probably guess what happened. He sucked. In 2006 nothing Trevor did worked. He walked around with his head hung down and had a horrible season. So Clint's field manager at the time traded him for a younger player. Clint had no say in this. One day Trevor was on the team; the next day he wasn't. The problem was, Trevor was such a big name in the league, had been the team's most successful player at one point, and was so well liked, the front office had been planning a Trevor Hall Day promotion. Trevor Hall bobble-head dolls had been ordered, and his parents were coming to town—it was going to be a great promotion. Then he got traded. Ironically, he was in town for Trevor Hall Day. Only he was wearing a different uniform, playing for the team to which he was traded.

Clint left the bobble-head dolls on a dock in Hong Kong, saving himself the thousand dollars it would have cost to ship them for a promotion they could no longer have. He still had the model, though, and tried to give it to Trevor's family, who had already arranged to be at the game. He remembers Trevor's sister staring daggers at him and Trevor's parents not being much happier. It was one of Clint's worst experiences. "Baseball can be a very cruel sport," he says. Trevor "was not injured. He had no reason not to have a spectacular year. But he didn't, and the ultimate insult was, he got traded."

The Trevor bobble-head fiasco is why Clint warns the host families who house players during the season not to get attached. In independent and some lower levels of the Minors, players, who are paid little, are often housed with a local family. Needless to say, the families often become fond of the young men staying in their homes. But becoming too fond, warns Clint, is dangerous. "Because if you do, one of these days you'll be disappointed, because by the definition of our league, it's not a matter of if, it's a matter of when, they're going to leave." And the hard thing is, the player replacing the player staying with the host family, "Guess where he's sleeping tonight?" Yep, that player will be staying in the same host family's house. So, Clint warns, you'd better be nice to him. But putting his advice into practice isn't always as easy as it sounds.

15. Closer to Ordinary

Fans of independent baseball like to say it is purer than affiliated ball. They claim the players are here because they love the sport, not because of the chance to obtain wealth and recognition. They say this is how baseball should be, how it used to be. They are right in some ways. The rules down here are more relaxed, less uniform. Players can be seen chewing tobacco and enjoying a beer with fans after a game. There is a public relations representative, but he is busy doing a hundred other things, so half the time the players and managers just handle the press themselves.

The closeness between players and their fans may be because the players are just one step away from ordinary. But it probably also has something to do with the fact that instead of bunking up on their own, they live in the homes of local families. Almost a thing of the past in the Minors, host families who house players are synonymous with independent baseball. And despite

Florence Freedom owner Clint Brown's warning that families not get attached to their players, the reality is that's why they do it, for the chance to get to know the players better, to create lasting attachments.

Last year Lori Snider attended a former player's wedding. Last weekend she attended another's college graduation. Both men lived with her when they played with the Freedom. Lori is forty-six and single, but she wasn't dating either man when they stayed in her three-bedroom home. Instead, she was serving as their host family, providing them with shelter and some food. In exchange she was given season tickets and a few other freebies.

Lori has served as a host mother as long as the program has existed and currently has three players staying with her, all of whom are trying to make the 2010 team. She has no children—just animals—can't cook, and works full-time as an accountant. But during spring training her mothering instinct kicks in, and she loads up on groceries so her players will have every advantage during the tryouts.

It is about halfway through spring training, a beautiful Saturday afternoon in mid-May, with no humidity and a slight breeze—perfect baseball weather. Lori and her mother, Shirley Brown, sit in the stands behind home plate at Champion Window Field, watching the first of today's two exhibition games against the Oakland County Cruisers. While they cheer on all Florence players, the mother and daughter save the biggest applause for the three players staying with Lori—Michael Manus, Daryl Jones, and Curt Marshall. Especially Curt Marshall, a catcher who attended church with the family last Sunday. "He's just a neat boy," says Shirley, who runs the host-family program with her sister, Bev Snider. "He came home the first night and emptied Lori's dishwasher."

Roseanna Koehler has another catcher staying in her home. He isn't playing too well, and when Roseanna's husband, Ron, shows up, he jokes they can sell his bed. That is fine by Lori and Shirley, because it means Curt has a better chance of staying.

Shirley laughs at the idea of host families not getting attached to their players. She knows better. Although she has never had a player in her home, she has heard from plenty of host families. "They'll call me and say 'Please don't touch my player,'" says Shirley. But it isn't something she can do anything about. She may boast that she has general manager Toby Rumfield's number on speed dial, but she knows it is just to take care of the ever-changing living situations, not to beg for a player's spot. Not even one of her daughter's players.

Two years ago, before Toby was managing the team, Shirley and Lori were leaving church one Sunday when they received cell phone messages saying both Lori's players had been released. Dinner plans were scratched, and the pair headed to Lori's house to say their good-byes. The players were packing, Lori was sobbing, and Shirley was helpless to do anything about it. Lori has seen more come—and go—since then, and still cries every time. The cure for her sadness is simple, say Shirley and Roseanna: "She gets another one."

And she has had many. This is Lori's and Roseanna's seventh year serving as host families. They are the only two families left who have been hosting since the program started. The second year the Freedom existed, the year the team had a stadium in town, is when Lori decided to host a player. Shirley thought she was crazy. The family had always loved attending baseball games. But letting a strange man live in your home, that was something else, something Shirley couldn't understand. But to Lori and Roseanna, it sounded like fun. There was no formal host-family program back then. But by the following year Shirley and her sister were running the show.

It isn't a paid position, unless you count the free tickets and T-shirts. But after getting to know the players who lived with Lori and Roseanna, it was one Shirley wanted to see succeed. Those players were "awesome," says Shirley, the kind of young men you would be proud to call son.

Shirley prepared for twenty-four players her first year. Then the manager told her he was bringing in extra players for spring training, a tryout period that lasts several weeks and is held at Champion Window Field. They put the extra players in a hotel.

It was a nightmare. When a player staying at the hotel got released, it became clear that the players that were expected to make the team were staying with host families, while the less likely prospects were housed at the hotel. Shirley didn't like that and made sure the following year that all the players were with host families, even if it meant placing three players in a home with only one bathroom. That is how Lori ended up with three players this season, even though she has only one-and-a-half baths. Curt and Daryl each have their own room, and Michael is in the basement on an air mattress. After all the cuts are made, the living arrangements will be reassessed, and Lori will be down to two players.

Roseanna and Ron started with six, but are already down to three. The "bloodletting" happened last Thursday. One player took off that night, another pulled out the next day, and the third is still with them. The two who left are from nearby Indiana. The straggler, Felix, is from Florida and is staying in town to see if he can get on with another team in the middle of the country before flying home. He recently landed a tryout in Washington, Pennsylvania, and plans to rent a car to get there. Luckily, he is twenty-five and so old enough to rent a car. In a league where age restrictions and other factors mean players tend to be between the ages of twenty-two and twenty-seven, that isn't always the case.

Felix's situation is far from unusual, explains Roseanna. The Koehlers once had a player from California stay with them two weeks while he tried to get on with another team. When you have to pay your own way to spring training, as many players on the Freedom do, she says, it is worth giving it your all in the area before buying a ticket home.

Then there were the two players from a team in Michigan who were traded to the Freedom—while in Florence for a series. They found out about the trade when they got off the bus in Florence and were told to report to the Freedom's clubhouse. When they showed up at the Koehlers' after the first game of the series, they had no toiletries. That's because when they had packed they had still belonged to the Michigan team and so packed for an away game, which meant staying in a hotel. Making matters worse, they had no money with which to buy any supplies because they now belonged to the Freedom and so were officially home and not out of town and thus had been given no travel money. To top it all off, after the series ended they had to take the bus back to Michigan with their former teammates in order to retrieve their things and drive their cars back to Florence. "That was just ugly," says Lori. "There are things that we don't necessarily agree with."

But that doesn't mean they won't take the players. The Koehlers are both pharmacists and have a spacious home, so they are often asked to house additional players until a more permanent placement can be made. The player staying with them might be a replacement for a player who has been released but has not actually left his host family yet, a player who is coming to town to try out during the season, or a player who has been released but has some loose ends to tie up before heading home.

Roseanna welcomes them all. When Roseanna was growing up her mother was in charge of an exchange-student program, and Roseanna thought having foreign students in her home was "the coolest thing." As an adult she has housed guest artists, baseball players, and visiting church groups. She likes the diversity the visitors expose her children to and keeps a map on which she marks the names and home states and countries of everyone who has stayed with them, from grandparents to shortstops.

There are far more ballplayers on the map than relatives. The guests also provide a great excuse for her to try out new recipes. If the ballplayers eat it, she figures her children, who are fourteen, twelve, and eleven, just might try it. While she knows some families are reluctant to take on players when they have teenage daughters in the house, she plans to keep hosting the players even after her eleven-year-old daughter reaches puberty. Because her daughter has grown up with players in the house, she doesn't think it will be a big deal.

Besides, once the season starts, the family doesn't see much of the players. They are at the ballpark playing games until late at night, sleep much of the morning, and then head back to the ballpark early in the afternoon. Their days off can be counted on one hand and sometimes don't even number that many. Plus, at the Koehlers' house they live in the basement with their own bathroom, so the need for interaction is small. Seven years ago the family might have played cards or chess with them, but now all the players bring their own gaming systems.

That isn't to say they don't talk. Ron is forty-eight and so about the right age to be dispensing fatherly advice to players in their early twenties. The players are a little more timid about confiding in Roseanna, who is also forty-eight. But she did have some really interesting religious conversations with one player. Roseanna is Protestant and enjoyed challenging the Catholic player to look more closely at what he had always simply accepted as true when it came to religion.

She went out of her way to warn another player, who was gorgeous, naive, and extremely popular with a group she refers to as the "bleacher chicks," not to get any of them pregnant. It's the kind of behavior you used to hear about in the Minors, the type of casual sex on display in the 1988 movie *Bull Durham*. While the host families all insist their players behave themselves, they don't shy away from talking about the bar scene and the cleat chasers there. With less of a reputation to uphold and less guidance from handlers, it is clear the players down here have a little more fun. Of course, it seems the local women, and this is coming from the other women, are to blame. The young men are fine specimens of humanity who go on to become upstanding citizens. One former player Roseanna housed wanted to become a policeman. Not long ago he contacted her to let her know she might be contacted by the police department where he had applied. Apparently, his prospective employer did not share his host family's confidence in his character and was suspicious of his frequent moves. The former player was hoping Roseanna might help explain things if they contacted her. One of Lori's former players also went into law enforcement.

While a few players make it to affiliated ball, very few make it to the Majors, and most of Lori's and Roseanna's former players are now married, with children and regular nine-to-five jobs. One of Lori's current players recently asked her opinion on an engagement ring he planned to present to his girlfriend. Lori was touched, and a little surprised, because she had never met the girl and had no idea what kind of taste she had.

Lori allows her players to invite long-term girlfriends to come for short stays, but won't let them bring home girls they pick up at the bar. While most of the players are single, a few have wives and occasionally even a child. It is up to the host families to decide how they handle overnight guests. On a spreadsheet Shirley lists the host families and a description of their homes and habits. The categories include bed size—"You don't want to put a six-foot-seven guy in a twin bed"—pets, smoking, children, and shirt size. The last is for the free host-family T-shirt they are given. The other categories are a guide to ensure that a first baseman who is allergic to dogs isn't placed in a home with three pooches and a tall chain-smoking pitcher isn't placed in a home with a twin bed and a family of nonsmokers.

The matches are usually pretty successful. Lori has had only one bad experience. From the start she didn't trust the guy. She could tell he snooped around in her bedroom. "I don't really have a whole lot of secrets, but I don't dust that well either, and I can tell" when things are moved, she says. He also didn't listen to her warning about not leaving food out because her greyhound would eat it. Later he tried to blame the dog for peeing on the guest mattress and comforter. Lori knew better. The dog had never peed on the bed, and, besides, it didn't smell like dog pee; it smelled like human pee. It happened after the player was released. Although Lori had nothing to do with his release, he felt she was in some way responsible, and so he left his mark. She knew something was wrong when he called to tell her he was leaving. He sounded angry at her and said something about how she already knew he was being let go. When she went home to wash his bedding, she says the stench was so bad "it just about knocked you down." Although there was little she could do after the incident occurred, word spread among the players, and it is rumored that it reached the new team he was playing for, and every time he went to bat the umpire struck him out. He has since been banned from the Frontier League in which the Freedom plays for other problems, a move that left Lori feeling vindicated.

The majority of the players, though, are good guys who know the host families are helping them and are very protective of them. Which is probably why no host family has ever quit because they didn't like it, says Shirley. There was one guy, she admits, but "we didn't like him either." The rest they lose because they move outside the eight- to ten-mile radius surrounding the ballpark Shirley requires of host families, get a divorce, or downsize their home. Then there was one woman who had a really nice house, but they found out from the player who stayed there that it was a mess on the inside. They didn't invite her back the next year.

Shirley uses her intuition—not background checks—in accepting families into the program. When a family responds to the radio announcement or website posting calling for host families, she makes a point of driving by their home to check out the neighborhood. If it is a place she isn't familiar with, or a family she doesn't know much about, she will invite them to lunch or dinner. "They don't know we're checking them out," she says.

The only person she remembers turning down outright was a woman in her forties who looked much younger—and acted it too—hanging around the guys at games and then going to bars with them afterward. "They call them cleat chasers, and every year there's somebody," she says. But there aren't any among this year's host families, just a doctor, an airline mechanic, a soon-to-be middle school principal, a flight attendant, a state representative, and three cops. The families vary in age, income, and experience—thirteen have done it before, and ten are new this year.

Then there are the players she matches them with. Shirley keeps a list of all of them on another sheet of paper. Quite a few names have already been crossed out; some of those have already left, but others have yet to be informed they are being let go. There is a picnic for the host families and players this afternoon, so the bad news will have to wait until after that, says manager Toby Rumfield. It isn't as callous as it sounds. It is just the reality of the situation.

There are six days until opening day, six days to whittle thirty players down to twenty-four. One of the best ways to evaluate players, to make sure they can perform under pressure, is in a game situation. That is one reason Toby brings so many players to spring training—so they can play intersquad games. At the start of spring training a little more than a week ago there were around forty-two players. The exhibition games being played today and tomorrow will go a long way toward cutting the thirty left down to twenty-four. "It's a cruel business is what it is," says Toby.

Toby isn't the type to spin things; he is a straightforward Texan. He may look a little rough, he may not sugarcoat his words, but his personality is gentle. He knows what it's like to be released, because when he was playing it happened to him—more than once. Even now, if he doesn't choose a winning team, he knows he is in danger of losing out on his current position. As undesirable as it may be, it is a regular paycheck, and for a guy without a college degree and three young children to support, that is worth a lot. It is also something he loves and something he can share with his two sons, who suit up and hang out with him during games.

The situation is nothing new for the players. Unless they are coming right out of college, most of them have been released before, says outfielder Billy Mottram. Billy was released by the

Chicago Cubs organization in 2008 and has been with Florence ever since. He knows what to expect. But even Billy can find the locker room a "little edgy" during spring training. He tries to stick to himself and not get too involved with who's staying and who's going. It's a good tactic in a sport where a competitor one year may end up a teammate the next. When he was released in 2008, Billy's first reaction was that it was time to get a job. "Time to start working, time to get in the real world," he says.

Not the world he had inhabited since he started playing baseball at the age of five in Haverhill, Massachusetts, just outside Boston. That world took him to Dowling College in Long Island. He was drafted his junior year, but after getting appendicitis and losing twenty pounds he opted to return to school for another year and went to the Chicago Cubs in the thirty-sixth round in 2007, his senior year. Being a senior, and so without the leverage of being able to go back to school another year, his signing bonus was small. He didn't mind, though. At that point all he wanted was a chance to play.

They sent him to the Boise Hawks in Idaho for Class-A Short-Season. Later he was assigned to the Class-A Daytona Cubs in Daytona Beach, Florida, where he finished the 2007 season batting a less than stellar .138. In the off-season he started having shoulder problems and spent a few months during the winter in rehabilitation. A little into spring training in 2008 he was released. Although his discharge didn't catch him totally by surprise, in addition to going to rehabilitation during the off-season, he had been working out with several guys who are now in the Majors and had expected to be given more of a chance. "But it's a business, and that's how things work, especially once you have some injuries and some arm problems," he says.

Billy was planning his entrance into the "real world" when

he got a call from the Freedom asking him to try out. It was an easy decision. He knew he could still play, and now he was being given a chance to prove it. That the chance was coming from an unaffiliated team was something he tried not to look at as a step down so much as a different path, one that he knows will make his road to the big leagues longer.

But it also means it is still possible, if not probable. Scouts can often be spotted in the stands. They are the guys taking notes and dressed in nice pants and shoes instead of shorts and flip-flops. Toby has told Billy there has been interest in him and moved him from second base to left field this season in the belief that he projects better as an outfielder.

In the end it won't make a difference, not this season. But they don't know that yet. Right now all they know is that there is no reason Billy shouldn't have an excellent season. Last season he batted .281, with twenty-three home runs, and had a team-leading thirty stolen bases in thirty-seven attempts. He led the team in runs batted in and runs scored. His goal this season is to hit .300 with anywhere from fifteen to twenty home runs, seventy to eighty runs batted in, and thirty to forty stolen bases.

And of course make it back into affiliated ball. Not that un-affiliated differs that much from the lower levels of affiliated. It still is a lot of sandwich meats and peanut butter and jelly served in the clubhouse and bunking up with strangers. In Idaho when he was with the Boise Hawks, Billy was housed with a Mormon family, which made for a few awkward weeks while he adjusted to their lifestyle. His current host-family situation is more relaxed—and familiar. He is living with the same single guy he lived with last season and the season before. Also living with them is infielder Johnny Welch. Billy and Johnny met in college when they used to play against each other and live about a half hour away from each other in Massachusetts in the off-season. When they have time off during the season they like to go to a local amusement park. "It's good to just kind of get away from the game a little bit, clear your mind," says Billy. "Because obviously baseball's a game of failure, you have to have a short memory in this game."

Billy has suffered enough disappointments and injuries to know better than to count on making a living in baseball forever. But he still enjoys it and has the enthusiasm and confidence to think he just might make a go of it a bit longer, even if that means working as a substitute teacher during the off-season. It isn't the kind of lifestyle conducive to relationships—too much travel and instability, too little pay—which may be why he hasn't had a serious girlfriend since college. All of which leaves him wondering, and people continually asking, "How long you gonna do this?"

That is what Tim Grogan would like to know. At almost twenty-six he is not even a year older than Billy, but more than a year separates them when it comes to the future. Tim mixes talk about making it back into affiliated ball with his fall wedding plans. He is a hometown boy who loves that his father can watch him play and that he is still playing. But he seems ready to move on. He has had countless last seasons. The only reason he is back this year is because he wanted to coach in the Freedom's academy, and to do that they told him he would need to play, explains his father, also Tim Grogan.

He doesn't like the senior-junior thing, doesn't really like the namesake thing at all, and blames his ex-wife for that. So he calls himself the first Tim Grogan and his son the second. But it isn't just the name the two share. The first Tim played college baseball at Northern Kentucky University. He even had some tryouts with professional teams but didn't make the cut. His son was just a baby when he picked up a toy bat. When he was a little older his mom hung a Wiffle ball for him to hit from the oak tree in their backyard. "I just loved to hit, ever since I was little," says the younger Tim.

He played three years at Western Kentucky University before being drafted by the Mets in the nineteenth round in 2005, his junior year. He signed for fifty thousand dollars and was assigned to the Brooklyn Cyclones for Class-A Short-Season. His season ended when he had to have surgery to repair bone spurs in his right elbow. The following year he was sent back to Brooklyn and later released. "I could see it coming," he says. "They had some younger prospects, like seventeen-year-olds, they were really pushing."

He took it as a sign to hang up his cleats and finish school. Then he heard from the Freedom. He knew the management, knew the area, and found it hard to pass up the chance to play professional baseball in his hometown. But even knowing all he did, the transition wasn't easy. "I really struggled my first year . . . I thought this must be a step down from where I've been, and it's really not," he explains. "It's really good baseball, and it's improved every year in this league."

By his second year he had made the adjustment mentally and physically and was ready to really commit to baseball again, when an old shoulder injury ended up requiring surgery. He took it as a sign that maybe he wasn't made for the game and should give it up for good. Then Toby took over managing the team and convinced him otherwise.

The following season started out really well, until he pulled his hamstring and had to sit out for two weeks. He came back, but he wasn't fully healthy, and mentally it was hard to play that way, he says. He ended up finishing the season batting .270, with twelve home runs and sixty runs batted in.

That was last season. Now he is back again looking for one more chance at a healthy season and a shot at getting back into affiliated ball. Although he knows he is no longer a prospect, that he is officially "an old guy" in this league, which requires most players to be under twenty-seven, as long as he can play, he can't give up that dream.

At the same time he knows not to take anything for granted, not even his chance to play unaffiliated ball. He has a new pair of shoes but has yet to bring them into the clubhouse. "I'm afraid I'll walk in there and bring them and 'See you later,'" he says. "I've been here, I know I'm liked here, but I'm still in the same boat as everybody else and have to earn a spot and show that I can still play. Because there's always hungry guys right behind you ready to step in." Hungry rookies so eager to play they will do so for six hundred dollars or so a month. As a veteran Tim makes more like sixteen hundred, but even that is hard to live on, especially if you have a family. That is one reason he returned to college part-time last year. He also took up coaching; he thinks that might be what he will do after he quits playing. Right now he waits tables at his mother's restaurant in the off-season.

During the season his father can be found at almost every game. "I wasn't the same hitter he is," says the elder Tim. "I could hit it a long way. I just couldn't hit it enough."

His son hasn't hit his stride yet this season, he says. But even when he does, it still might not be enough. Once you get to a certain level, a lot of guys are just as good as you are, and unless you get the breaks, you don't make it, says the elder Tim. "I was just thinking of that today, how lucky you have to be, how lucky these guys have to be, to make it to the Major Leagues, not only to have talent, but to stay healthy enough to do it," he says. He never made it that far and instead manages a transportation company. His son may have the talent, but he has never stayed healthy long enough to find out. Now he is running out of time.

The men sitting on a low wall up behind the stands along the right-field line probably wouldn't like him as much if he had. They prefer the Minor Leagues and unaffiliated baseball to the Majors. They can afford the tickets and access the athletes better at the lower levels, says Lawson Chapman, a forty-six-year-old jeweler. With the Freedom, Lawson can even afford season tickets. But he is seldom in his seat. Instead, he sits on the wall blocking off a bar on the concourse with a small group of men who engage in air-horn wars, smoke cigars on occasion, and always tip the bartenders well, or so they say. They are known as the "Wall Rats," a name they were given by a girl who told them they looked like a bunch of rats sitting on a wall. They never thought to change it. Instead, they put it on T-shirts, hats, and even a banner that hangs above their wall. "Next year it's going to be pajamas," says Lawson.

As Lawson talks, Liberty, the team's eagle mascot, hits him on the butt with a plastic bat. Without missing a beat, Lawson taps Liberty on the beak. Liberty in turn removes Lawson's baseball hat, places it dramatically on the wall, wiggles his feathered butt, and takes a seat on the hat. "Hey, give me the thing," says Lawson, retrieving his hat.

Other members of the Wall Rats include Joe "Mojo" Morris, a seventy-five-year-old retired truck driver, and Mike Luken, a concrete guy wearing suspenders and smoking a cigar. Aaron Luken, Mike's second cousin, is not yet old enough to be an official Wall Rat, but still young enough to find being the group's gopher fun. He is fourteen and counting the years until he is twenty-one, the age at which he can officially join the pack.

Then there are the groupies, the nonmembers who stop by the wall every game, including last year's Freedom intern who also happens to be this year's Freedom accountant. A little guy with a beard, he was at the field early this morning, wearing a catcher's outfit for a commercial the team filmed advertising one-dollar hot dogs. At this level the line between workers, players, and fans is crossed regularly. That is one of the things Lawson loves about Freedom players. "These guys are trying to make the Majors, they dream of the bigs, they hustle, they work a lot harder," he says. "When you go give them a baseball or something to sign, they're like, 'You actually want my autograph?'" Yeah. He does.

16. Strike Two

Being an independent team is the first strike against the Freedom. Chuck Hildebrant is the second. Or maybe he is really the first. Even today, almost a decade after it all began, and a half decade or so since it ended, the ghost of Chuck haunts the team.

It wasn't always that way. When Jeff Hollis began his job as Freedom general manager in September 2002 it was a dream come true. When he was a kid growing up in Florence in the 1980s and '90s, the closest thing to professional baseball was the Reds, who played across the river in Cincinnati at Riverfront Stadium (now Cinergy Field). He went to about thirty games there every summer. It is this interest that helps explains why he ended up working in baseball despite studying history in college. And notwithstanding an internship with the Indianapolis Indians, which included his keeping score during one game without being able to see—he lost his contacts—he landed a job with the Louisville RiverBats after graduating from college in 1999.

Jeff was in charge of media and public relations in Louisville when he left a few years later to become the Freedom's general manager. He resigned from the Freedom staff on April 1, 2003, just a little more than six months after starting. A suit was filed. Jeff will say no more. Newspaper accounts pick up where he leaves off. They report that Jeff sued the team's ownership group over salary and benefits he said he never received.[1]

When it comes to the history of professional baseball in Florence, there is pretty much only one thing on everyone's mind—the troubling history of the Florence Freedom. There may have been semiprofessional teams in the area before. There may have been professional teams in nearby cities like Covington, Maysville, and Newport. But all of that is overshadowed by the scandal that haunted the Freedom's first years.

It begins in 2001 on an encouraging note with talk of the independent Frontier League expanding to Florence. The league had successfully started teams in other areas close to Major League markets, and it seemed something similar could be done in Florence. Northern Kentucky Professional Baseball Ltd. agreed to build a stadium on thirty-three acres of land leased from the city. The partnership's biennial lease payments would cover up to half of the $5 million the city would pay for the property, and their managing partner, Chuck Hildebrant, personally guaranteed he had the means to build the $8 million (or so) stadium.[2]

Newspaper accounts were almost breathless in their excitement over team-name possibilities, sponsorship deals, and the new ballpark. Former Cincinnati Reds third baseman Chris Sabo was named team manager, and the city's mayor bought season tickets. Then things started to change, construction on the stadium fell behind, and there was still no name and, in fact, no team. By late May 2003 Chris Sabo had resigned. The stadium was not complete, and the team's first season was played in Hamilton, Ohio.

By midsummer 2004 construction on the stadium, which had opened but was still not finished, stopped after several contractors filed liens against Northern Kentucky Professional Baseball. By the end of July 2004 ten contractors had filed liens against the team totaling $3 million.[3] Around the same time the Frontier League took over management of the team so the ownership group could focus on fixing the financial problems.

Then the City of Hamilton filed a lawsuit, claiming the ownership group had not paid an old utility bill and owed the city more than $3,000. By August the City of Florence was seeking to evict the team, based on at least eighteen lease violations, including unpaid rent.[4] By early September Northern Kentucky Professional Baseball had declared bankruptcy.

It gets even worse. The FBI began investigating how Chuck Hildebrant, a 20 percent owner in the baseball group, financed the stadium's construction. The City of Florence, and banks through which Chuck secured loans for the stadium's construction, claimed that he grossly overstated his financial situation and even falsified financial statements that were used to prove his wealth. In January 2005 Chuck pleaded guilty to bank fraud, filing a false income-tax report, and making a political contribution in the name of another person. He was later sentenced to five years in federal prison.

That is the legacy Clint Brown inherited when his purchase of the team was approved in December 2004. About $1.3 of the $3 million he paid for the team plus $600,000 from the city went toward paying contractors who agreed to accept about half of the $3.8 million they were owed. The city waived the team's first lease payment due in 2004 and deferred the two payments due in 2005.[5]

As for Jeff Hollis, he thinks it is wonderful his hometown has a baseball team. But despite frequent trips back to visit family and friends, he doesn't attend games. He never returned to baseball and now makes a living writing grants for Goodwill Industries of Kentucky. He uses a Douglas Adams quote to sum up the path he took. "I may not have gone where I intended to go, but I think I ended up where I needed to be."

Thanks to Chuck there are still baseball fans like Jeff missing from the Freedom's stands. Because of what Chuck did, the team has had to win over not just those who think independent ball is a joke, but also those who feel betrayed by the deception on which he founded the Freedom.

17. A Long Way to Go

About halfway through summer the baseball season seems as if it will stretch on forever. Officially, the Freedom's season is shorter than that of most Minor League teams. Unofficially, it lasts long past any excitement the players and coaches once showed. They are far from where they want to be, and the longer the season goes without them moving, the further they are from their desired destinations. The travel, the tedium, and the low pay make for an exhausting existence even when you have hope that things will improve. As time passes and that hope dims, fatigue sets in.

Freedom manager Toby Rumfield and pitching coach Pedro Flores don't bother talking. Instead, they text faraway family members, a brief escape from the monotony of their existence. They are hunkered down over a small table at Cracker Barrel, a short stop on their latest road trip that began today and includes a three-day series in Evansville, Indiana, followed by another in Marion, Illinois.

Toby doesn't look much like a baseball manager, outfitted in a black T-shirt with a skull on it and army fatigue shorts. The ubiquitous polo shirts worn in the Minors are absent in independent baseball. Without them, dressed in T-shirts and sweats, it is hard to distinguish the players from their fellow road travelers.

Of course, there are still some barriers. I am not allowed on the bus and must trail behind in my own car. But instead of having to clear everything through the media representative, I am able to talk directly to Toby. In part the casual arrangements are a result of the media flak having left to take a job in China midseason. There is no doubt a story there, but the one I am after is with Toby, so I just call his cell phone. Turns out he is better at texting. He gets in touch at the last minute, when they are already on the road.

He has a good excuse. It is mid-July, and they have just come off the four-day All-Star break, but it wasn't much of a break for Toby. It began with his traveling to Illinois for the All-Star Game and then to Indiana to watch his oldest son, T. J., compete in the Continental Amateur Baseball Association World Series with his under-ten team. Toby arrived home last night, mowed the lawn, and got back on the road again this morning. "It never stops," he says, sipping his iced tea.

It's around noon, and they are in Corydon, Indiana, about halfway through their three-plus-hour bus ride. Toby has traveled this route many times before, stopping at this same old-fashioned-style country-cooking eatery just as many times. But aside from knowing the exit number, he is lost. "I couldn't tell you where we're at right now," he says.

Indiana, Kentucky, he doesn't know. All he knows is they are on the way to their next series, and this is a good place to stop for food. He is more confident about the choice of restaurant than he is about his team. He admits they have been up and down, good one week, bad one week, good one week, bad one week. On the good side, Tim Grogan was named most valuable player at the All-Star Game, making it four years in a row that Florence has had an MVP in the game. The bad news no doubt includes the four consecutive losses they suffered before finally winning their last game ahead of the All-Star break.

Toby insists he isn't offering excuses when he chronicles the injuries they have suffered. The team's top pitcher, Everett Saul, spent time on the disabled list in June, and another veteran pitcher, Andy Clark, also spent the early part of the season injured. Now Toby is trying to regroup, get some new starting pitching in, and hopefully see some better results the second half of the season.

He knows he will need it if he wants to return to his job next year. And although it isn't exactly well paid—his wife makes probably double what he does—and it isn't in affiliated ball, he likes it. There are advantages to being overlooked and out of the spotlight. The main one is control. Unlike in the Minors where you have little say over the composition of your team, Toby makes all the decisions. He recruits, signs, and plays who he wants. And that goes for the coaching staff as well, which now includes Pete Rose Jr. Toby and Pete Rose Jr. were roommates when they were both playing in the Minors and have stayed in touch over the years. Last year Pete Rose Jr., who is forty, retired after spending more than twenty years playing in professional baseball, mostly in the Minors.

While his father may hold the record for all-time Major League career hits, Pete Rose Jr.'s big league record is short. He had one stint in the Majors in 1997 with the Reds, hitting .143 in eleven games. He was nowhere near close to achieving his father's three World Series rings, three batting titles, and countless other honors and awards. He did, however, have a little trouble with the law, kind of like his dad. In 2005 he pleaded guilty to a drug charge and was later sentenced to one month in prison and several months of home detention.

But doping aside, no one knows baseball like a Pete Rose. That is why Toby offered the younger one a job as hitting coach last month. Pete Rose Jr. lives just across the river from Florence in Cincinnati, where his father spent most of his career and where he had his brief stint in the Majors. He isn't here now because of an earlier scheduled vacation, so we won't hear from him just yet. There has to be something left to look forward to this season, and Pete Rose Jr. may be it. Toby for one has high hopes. "I hate to say this," says Toby, "but he's gonna be a lot better coach than he ever was a player. He's just got the knack for communicating with people, socializing, getting people to understand, buy into what he's preaching." That last part is the biggest thing about coaching and managing: getting players to buy into what you're saying.

And in this league you have to say it over and over again, adds Pedro. There is a lot of instruction, a lot of teaching, and sometimes Pedro wishes he could just get out there and do it himself. "Toby, he's told me about that," says Pedro, who is from California. "He said there's gonna be a lot of times you want to go out there, 'Just give me the ball,' and pitch, but we can't, obviously. We're the coaches." It's a new role for Pedro. Until recently he was still playing. In 2008 he played with an independent team, but he played affiliated ball earlier and in Mexico. As a foreigner in Mexico he was paid $10,000 a month in cash, plus room and board, and $100 a day in meal money, he says.

Coaching for the Freedom doesn't quite add up to all that. As they finish off their biscuits and drinks, Toby and Pedro each pull out an envelope filled with $20 bills. As coaches they get $25 a day in meal money when they are on the road, $5 more than the players. But it doesn't work out quite so well, says Toby, because the players tip the clubhouse manager $1 a day, while coaches and managers tip more.

Unlike in the lower levels of affiliated ball, in independent ball the home team usually offers an after-game meal to players. Often it is concession food, but it is food all the same. When they are home Florence players get their after-dinner meal from local restaurants as part of a barter deal. Before the game they usually get sandwiches in the clubhouse, which is good because $20 doesn't go too far, says Toby. "I just had lunch for $14.20. If they got the same thing I got, it's over," he says.

It's over anyway, at least this stop on the road. Almost exactly an hour after pulling into Corydon, the players make their way back to the bus. They shuffle on, dressed in sweats, T-shirts, and sandals and holding snacks and plastic drink containers. On the bus they settle down with pillows, blankets, and headphones. On the floor are coolers and sometimes a player or two.

That is where outfielder Billy Mottram spent the trip. Cocky and cute, Billy is a bit of a ham. He jokes that he tries to make a deal with the guy sitting next to him that allows one player to sleep across the two seats and the other to sleep on the floor. Billy usually ends up on the floor, snuggled on top of his blanket.

An hour or so later, when they arrive at the EconoLodge right off the highway in Evansville, he waits in the lobby as Toby and Pedro pass out room keys. When they have their keys the players exit as quickly as they entered, heading to their rooms to nap, shower, and relax in the few hours they have before getting back on the bus and heading to the field.

One player stays in the lobby talking on his cell phone. He says something about the impossibility of having children when the person he is talking to, and whom he is supposedly in a relationship with, works at a camp and he is at a hotel trying to hit balls over a fence. That's infielder Johnny Welch, and a little later he joins Billy and Andy Clark for lunch. Johnny already ate a chicken sandwich at Wendy's when they stopped in Corydon, but he is tall and lean and doesn't pass up a meal. Plus, he and Billy are pretty much a pair. Their choice is simple—Culver's or White Castle. They choose Culver's and head out on a path that takes them over some dirt, through an unfinished field, and around a parking lot or two. At one point a woman unloading sandbags from her car offers them a nice warm-up of carrying the bags. They decline but offer up the players trailing just behind them. Those guys are headed to the gym and need a warm-up, they say. Then they walk on, already sweating in the stifling ninety-plus-degree heat and humidity.

Last season they stayed at a different hotel, one that Billy thinks may have been torn down or gone out of business. That one was closer to the ballpark and downtown Evansville and had a lot more dining options within walking distance. This one is in the middle of shopping mall sprawl. There are no sidewalks here, no real way of getting from one place to another when you're on foot like they are. Usually, their lack of transportation on road trips isn't much of a problem, but here it is isolating. "This hotel, it's like we're stuck on an island . . . pretty much away from everything," says Billy.

They're away from everything in other ways as well. It's a Friday afternoon, and most people are working. Billy and his companions don't have to worry about that until tonight. Other young men their age might be making plans to take their girlfriends out to dinner this weekend. Billy has only seen his girlfriend a few times this season. They know each other from college, and over the All-Star break he went to visit her in Toledo, Ohio. "We've been off and on, I guess since college, trying to make it work," he says. He doesn't have to add that the strange schedule and traveling that accompany his job put a huge strain on a relationship. And that holds true not just for girlfriends. In independent ball sometimes it's a revolving door, explains Billy, with guys coming and going, making it hard to build any kind of team chemistry. Just when you start building a relationship with a guy, he gets sent home, and next thing you know there's another guy in the locker next to you.

A core group has stayed, including Johnny, Billy's housemate in Florence, and they keep trying to build on that core. On the road Billy and Johnny try not to room together so they don't get sick of each other, but they still tend to grab meals together, like they are now. As they walk slowly in the heat, Johnny continues to talk on the phone.

Billy's season hasn't gone quite like he hoped, and no matter what happens now he knows it won't be enough to make up for what has been lost. The seven bases he stole and two home runs and twelve runs batted in he had last month aren't what he needs to reach his season goal of at least fifteen home runs, seventy runs batted in, and thirty stolen bases. There were some injuries—a cracked bone in his left hand, a sprained ligament in the thumb of the same hand. It's also his first season in the outfield. But the transition hasn't been bad, especially once he was assigned to center field, where he feels he can get a lot truer reads than in left field, where he played one game. He still has to work on his first step and reads off the bat, but otherwise his speed is good enough that he can get by out there, he says. As for batting, he thinks Pete Rose Jr.'s coaching is helping him swing a bit better. "I kind of can relate to him a little bit more being left-handed," he says. "Because he's a left-hand hitter as well, so we kind of have similar swings, which helps me out a lot."

Pete also does a lot of videotaping, which has helped Billy see what he is doing. In the speed of the game, when you are at the plate, it can be hard sometimes to feel it, says Billy. But if you can see it on video and kind of break it down and see what you're doing and not doing, it helps. Just like he's not really sure what happened to the hotel where they used to stay, Billy's not too sure what happened to the hitting coach they had before Pete Rose Jr.

At Culver's Billy orders a cheddar bacon cheeseburger and heads to the corner booth they sat at their last trip here. Johnny ends his phone call, Andy grabs an *Evansville Courier & Press*, and they all take a seat at the table, which wobbles exactly like it did the last time they were here. Today the food tastes good. But by tomorrow they'll be tired of it. That's what happens when there isn't a lot of variety.

Billy mixes mayonnaise in with his ketchup, joking that he is trying to eat as healthy as he can. He was rushing when he packed this morning and may have forgotten a few things. Last road trip he forgot underwear. That was the road trip the hotel put an older couple in among all the players. They had just gotten back from a game one night, and the older woman was already yelling at them to be quiet, says Johnny. "I don't think she really understood," he says, adding that because of the odd hours players keep, hotel managers usually separate them from "normal civilians."

They don't talk a lot at lunch. Starting today they will play twenty-four games in a row. As they finish up they contemplate ice cream, but decide against it, figuring it is so hot outside the ice cream will melt on the walk back to the hotel. The heat is nothing like the heat they experience at home playing on turf. Before the break they played a couple of games when the temperature was in the high nineties, which is substantially hotter on the turf, says Billy, "so your feet are like burning up, sweating like crazy."

After lunch Billy convinces the guys to head to a gas station so he can buy a can of snuff. It's a habit he acquired in college, and while you can get fined for it in the Minors, in this league, he says, they don't really mind. Getting to the gas station may be even more dangerous than his habit. With no sidewalks, they decide to dart across two lanes of traffic and walk in the median of a busy street. They travel single file, balancing on the cement island as cars and trucks whiz by on either side of them.

Inside the gas station shop, Billy eyes the frozen dinners, asking his friends, "No microwave, right?" They don't bother to answer, and he moves on to another aisle. Andy loads up on sunflower seeds and candy, Johnny on milk, Mountain Dew, and water; Billy gets two cans of smokeless tobacco and two little bottles of an energy drink. Outside the gas station they contemplate their options and somehow end up with a safer route back, until they get to the weed-covered ditch in front of their hotel.

"Ah, Billy, now we got to do this," says Johnny. "What kind of thing lives in here?"

"I don't know, but I wish I had sneakers on," says Billy.

Andy jokes that he is hungry again. Later today, tomorrow, the next day, they'll do it all over again. Then they'll do something similar in another town.

"We never know what day it is," says Johnny. "We know what time the bus is and where we're going next."

Today they don't need to be on that bus again for another

hour or two, so they head back to their rooms. Meanwhile, Tim Grogan has just left his room, following a nap. Dressed in sweatpants and a Goofy T-shirt, he is still a little groggy as he talks about a season that overall is turning out pretty well, at least for him. Tim is quieter and more reserved than his teammates. He talks about his success sparingly, as if it might disappear if he harps on it too long. He keeps his face hidden behind a perpetual unshaven scruff and his eyes lowered.

He started out really well, and before the All-Star break he was batting .307, with seven home runs and twenty-one runs batted in. Although his average has slid a little the past few weeks, he is still getting on base and doing things to help the team out. Toby moved him to the number-two slot in the batting lineup, trying to get him on base for some of the team's bigger hitters.

Then there was the All-Star Game. It wasn't the first time he was invited, but it was the first time he actually got to go. Last time he had a torn labrum in his shoulder and had to turn them down. This time, he says, "it was great. It was awesome." It's a little different, he explains, because you're put with a team you don't know, aside from any of your teammates who also made the team. It's competitive, but mostly everyone's out to have a lot of fun. After scoring a home run he was pretty sure he was going to be named MVP and was thrilled, especially with it "probably" being his last year.

Even now, with his college courses starting up again in a little more than a month, he won't say for sure this is his final season. Even if he did, it might not mean much to those who know him. Back in Florence his fiancée, Katie Sparrow, said she was a little surprised when Tim told her he was going to play again this season. "Because he had told me he was done, I prepared for that, and when the plans changed, I was kind of turned off a little bit," she said. She got over it, though. She is from the Florence area and has been with Tim since his college years, so she is used to the roller-coaster ride that is professional baseball. The biggest dip probably came after he was released from affiliated baseball and before he decided to play with Florence. It was their second year living together, she said, and "it was really hard living with him and him living that disappointment of him being released."

The disappointment didn't ever really go away, but it lessened, and in time they settled into a life of his playing for Florence and her working as a hair stylist. This season she finally got to see him play in the All-Star Game. She has also been busy planning their wedding. Tim just took care of the guy things, which include a bachelor party in Charlotte, North Carolina, at the end of September. There will be a lot of boating, fishing, golfing, and watching of football on that trip. He asked his father to be his best man.

At school he is taking easy classes, like finite math, calculus, and econometrics. His classes are only on Tuesdays and Thursdays, so he won't miss too many. But he still needs to contact his professors and let them know that when the team is on the road in late August, he will miss a few classes.

Then there is the part-time job offer he received from the Freedom that really changed his plans. It's a front-office position that puts him in charge of amateur baseball, which basically is all aspects of Freedom business that is not the professional team—the high school and youth teams that use the field, several new youth teams playing under the Freedom banner, the baseball academy, and, of course, like everyone in the front office, ticket sales.

Freedom owner Clint Brown approached Tim about the position before the season started, but it wasn't until June that

Clint came back with an actual offer. It's a win-win for both of them, says Tim. Clint gets someone with a lot of experience, and Tim gets to start a new career in his off-season, or, as he adds, laughing, "my retired season, I guess you could call it." It seems almost too good to be true, and in the end it may be, but that isn't something Tim knows yet. Now he just has to finish the second half of the season. "It can get to be a little bit of a drag physically and mentally, so you kind of have to find a way to maybe do something different one day, or break up your routine, just so you don't get bored with it," he says.

We're not talking anything drastic, no big nights out or big-ticket purchases, just not working out when you're on the road, sleeping a little later some mornings, little things like that. And at this point, enjoying the forty-eight games he has left in what may well be his last season of professional baseball. It sounds like a lot, but it goes quickly, so he is just trying to enjoy every day. "Last Evansville trip. It's a last everything, I guess," he says.

Retiring from driving trucks for Caterpillar wasn't really the same kind of last time for Richard Collins. He's still driving, only now he is driving the Freedom. He is based out of Peoria, Illinois, and drives the coach down to Florence the day before a road trip so he has a little rest before taking the team on the road. It is his job not just to get them to wherever they are playing, but also once there to get them to and from the field every day and sometimes to meals afterward. His company likes to keep the same driver and coach with a team, but in the past he's hauled other teams as well, even been with some teams so strict on punctuality that the coach instructed him to leave the starting pitcher at the hotel when he wasn't at the bus on time. "I think he had to walk to the ball diamond, which was two to three miles away," says Richard.

That was with an affiliated team. Even the bus driver, it seems, draws a clear line between Minor League players and their independent counterparts. The Minor League players are more disciplined: they don't wear shorts on road trips, they have room checks at night, and they are so quiet on the bus you can barely tell they are there, he says. No doubt they would also be more guarded than to tell a female reporter that they once forgot to pack underwear for a trip, as Billy did earlier with a sheepish grin. And they might not forget their equipment on the bus, as Freedom players frequently do. Richard routinely waits about fifteen minutes after dropping the team at the stadium for just that reason. Then he'll get something to eat before returning to watch the game.

He often sits up top, out of the way, but at this field he likes to sit behind home plate. The field is old, but draws big crowds. The entire stadium is covered, and the seats are wooden and painted green. Outside it is brick. The ballpark is quaint enough to have set the scene for much of the 1992 movie *A League of Their Own*. It's a nice setting if you have to have a thirteen-inning game, which Florence loses to the Evansville Otters, 8–7. Florence couldn't hold its 5–0 lead, and Evansville won it in the bottom of the thirteenth, leaving the first of Tim Grogan's last road games in Evansville a loss. Still, he has forty-seven more games to go, and two more here in Evansville.

18. Back to Reality

How do players know when it is time to give up on their dream of playing professional baseball, time to say good-bye to the road, the clubhouse, and the crowds? The truth is they don't. One day they just stop playing. It is a decision only they can make. In the six years Katie Sparrow has been with her fiancé, Tim Grogan, that is the biggest thing she has learned about baseball and the men who play it. "It is in these guys' blood," she says. "And if you don't let it ride out, I don't want to be the one that he's mad at ten years down the road because I nagged at him to stop playing."

There may be fewer incentives to stay in the game at this level, but that doesn't make the decision to leave any easier. Tim has wrestled with it for years. Now, as it comes to the close of what he said would be his final season, his family wonders if they can believe him. His father, Tim Grogan the elder, plans to watch his son's last professional baseball game. But, he adds with a laugh, he watched his son's last professional game last year as well.

This time Tim the younger says he is pretty sure he is done. There is a week left in the season, but he isn't thinking about the end of baseball as much as his college classes and a new job. Classes started last week, and Tim is having trouble keeping up, what with road trips that take him away for days at a time and night games that interfere with his two evening classes. Then there is his wedding and the youth team he has already started coaching as part of his new gig working with the Freedom amateur baseball program. He won't get a break from it all until his fall break from school, right before his new job kicks into full gear and right after his wedding. It's no wonder that he is looking forward to his honeymoon in Florida and "getting to lay on the beach and relax for a little while."

But first he has to finish the season. And complete his personal goal of staying healthy and playing in all ninety-six games. After tonight's game he will have seven to go. He is pretty pleased that he has made it this far without injury, but otherwise is disappointed in how the season has played out for him and the team. He'll finish the season with a .280 batting average, twelve home runs, forty-eight runs batted in, and a showing in the league's All-Star Game. But he rates his own season by how well the team does, and the team has not done well. They just never got hot, he says. They are ranked fifth out of the Frontier League West Division's six teams. "It's a bad way to go out," says his father.

It is the worst season he has watched since his son joined the team four years ago. They are playing so badly that Tim the elder has even started sitting down, instead of standing and cheering like he usually does. Still, he isn't ready for it to end—the season, or his son's playing days. He has been watching Tim play baseball since he was eight years old, and he could do it every night. But, he adds, "You got to quit at some point in time. You have to make a real living." As for him, he'll probably watch more Cincinnati Reds games on television next summer. This summer he still has a few more of his son's games to catch and plans to travel to Normal, Illinois, with his brother next weekend to catch Tim's last game. At least he thinks it will be Tim's last game. Katie is pretty sure it will be. Last year, she wasn't as convinced he was done. "I think he said he was because that's what he thought he should do," she says.

This year is different. She hopes. But even if it isn't, and Tim for some reason decides to play again, she'll leave that up to him. She attends almost all the home games, sitting with the girlfriends and wives of other players. She even cuts the hair of some of the Freedom staff. Her own hair is long and brown and straight, kind of like her build—lean and tan.

Even with Tim playing in their hometown, it doesn't mean she sees him all that much. It's more like they see each other in passing. He is on the road a lot, and then when he is home, he is getting in at three in the morning and wanting to sleep until two in the afternoon. Any kind of normal routine is impossible. As is any family summer vacation spent together. Instead, year after year, she goes to Florida with her family while Tim stays behind to play baseball. Next summer they'll be able to take their first family vacation together and, she jokes, have so much free time together they won't know what to do. In reality she knows it won't turn out quite like that because Tim's new job will still be in baseball, keeping him busy during the season, just not as busy as when he was playing.

There will be regrets, achievements not reached. But there will also be a Tim Grogan bobble-head doll. Tim wasn't really a big fan of the idea when his mother first told him about the bobble head, but now he is glad her restaurant helped sponsor the doll. The company that made it sent him three images to choose from—one had a frown, one had a smile, and he can't remember what the third looked like. He went with the one that had a little bit of a grin, the one he felt looked the most like him. They still sell the grinning Tim with his trademark scruff at the gift shop. He is the local boy who made it big—but not big enough. His dream, like so many players' dreams, was to play in the Major Leagues. He never did. Still, he hasn't fully given up on it. He plans to continue in baseball, and ten years down the road he might be coaching eighteen-year-olds and helping them get to the big leagues. "So I think there's other ways I can make my dream, even though I haven't personally done it myself," he says. "Kind of have new goals and ambitions to help others get there."

Randy Blaker is just getting into the game. He sits outside the Freedom clubhouse, rubbing mud onto shiny new baseballs. Not just any mud, but Mississippi mud, purchased online and shipped to him here, in Florence, so he can rub it on the game balls, thereby providing pitchers with a firmer grip over the balls. The importance of using Mississippi mud, and not any other kind of mud, is just one of the many things Randy has learned this season, his first working as a clubhouse manager in professional baseball.

Back in May he was digging up clay from the patch of lawn in front of the clubhouse, mixing it with water and sugar and smearing it on the balls. When the umpires learned what he was using, they laughed. Then they told him to get some Mississippi mud. They said something about the water flowing differently, and Randy bought it, and he has been buying Mississippi mud online ever since. He thinks the balls feel grainier and less sticky now and says the pitchers have noticed a difference.

His job is filled with a lot of little things like that: making sure the uniforms are ready for game day, the bats and balls are in order, and everyone has a towel. When players need a ride to the airport, he acts as chauffeur. And when they return from a bad road trip—a frequent occurrence this season—he tries to lift their spirits by posting inspirational quotes in the locker room. Right now a Vince Lombardi message is on display: "The spirit, the will to win, and the will to excel are the things that endure. These qualities are so much more important than the events that occur." There are some other inspiring quotes, and some that the players have turned into raunchier messages as well. Not the kind of thing Randy probably came across in the finance job he held before this season. He did that for three years and was losing his mind being inside all the time. So he went back to working in sports, which is what he started out doing back in college when he was offered a spot in equipment management instead of on the football team. He had planned to become a sports agent, but after an internship in Las Vegas he got sidetracked by a finance job back here in the Florence area. Now he is thirty-one and thinking about going down the baseball path.

Pete Rose Jr. never had to think about his path. A half hour or so before the game he is still in the batting cage, throwing balls to Johnny Welch. Between tosses he urges Johnny to stay down. "That's the thing. Tonight you got to get down on them, but the whole thing is your first at bat. I don't know if you really feel it," Pete says as he starts to pick up balls. "I do," Johnny replies.

A few minutes later Pete is in uniform and headed to the field. The "kids" are good and eager to learn, he says, "but playing for twenty years, I still miss it. They say that this is kind of a substitute for not playing. I still haven't found that out yet." He hadn't really intended to get into coaching so quickly. He had really hoped to take the summer off and just spend some time being a dad to his three-year-old daughter and five-year-old son. But when the offer came up, it was hard to turn down. He lives less than a half hour from the field, so he still gets to tuck the kids in at night and wake them up in the morning. Plus, working with his old roommate Toby has been fun.

But he doesn't plan to repeat it. Next year he hopes to be working in affiliated baseball. Toby doesn't doubt Pete will be a big league manager one day, just like his father. Pete is careful to point out it won't be his father's name that gets him there; it will be his experience playing in everything from the Major Leagues to independent ball, from Nicaragua to Mexico. "Because, sure enough, you got to get in the cage, and got to open your mouth, and you got to teach them something, so I think my knowledge is probably going to overtake my name," he says.

As for that name, it's the coolest thing in the world being named after his father, his idol, and he is proud to have it, he says. He named his own son Peter Edward Rose III, after his father. But he says he also named him after himself and calls him P. J., for Pete Rose Jr., so he doesn't have to deal with all the fan abuse he doesn't deserve if he ever decides to play baseball. "If I'm a betting man, which I'm sure I am, I'd probably say yes," he'll play baseball, says Pete. And, Pete adds, why wouldn't he, when he has the genes they have? In the next breath Pete insists he himself is a normal son with a normal dad. "The only difference is my dad's got more hits than your dad does, and I can say that about anybody's," he says. Then he steps onto the field.

In the stands the Wall Rats are gathered around their wall.

Above their heads is a banner with the original five Wall Rats drawn on it. Lawson Chapman's rat is toward the middle of the pack, a round little rat with a baseball bouncing off his head. It is the same image that is shown on the back of Lawson's brand-new Wall Rats T-shirt and a reminder of the game at which he was hit by a ball in a more vulnerable location on his lower body. Today is their first day wearing the new T-shirts, and it also marks their annual tailgate party, which started at the park quite a few hours prior to the game. It's an early game tonight, 6:05 p.m. on a Saturday, the team's last Saturday game and second-to-last home game. But Lawson and his wife are already showing signs of wear and have taken to lounging in their lawn chairs instead of sitting on the famous wall.

In their place on the wall are two foam rats, each about a foot or so tall. Lawson pulls out a camera and shows a photo of the foam rats posing in front of a mini coffin, a stunt they put together for the Freedom's "Dying to Get In" promotion a few days back. The idea was to give away an actual funeral, but the funeral home backed out at the last minute and the giveaways were of a smaller order. Surprisingly, it was not the first time a baseball team had a funeral giveaway promotion.

Lawson missed only one game this season, and that was a day game that he couldn't make because he had to work. After tomorrow there will be no more games to attend, but that isn't really the end of the Wall Rats. They have been spotted cheering on the local women's roller-derby team.

When the season ends Lori Snider; her mother, Shirley Brown; and her aunt, Bev Snider, will all switch from the host-family gig to judging horse competitions. All three judge cross-country jumping, even though the type of riding they enjoy involves the horse's feet staying on the ground considerably more. They'll be so busy with that, work, and other volunteer jobs, they joke that they won't have time to notice the end of the season. But they will. At home Lori's computer room will go back to being her computer room and not Curt Marshall's room. He was her favorite this season, and he is the only player who has stayed with her throughout. Tonight she is wearing the Freedom shirt he signed. Tomorrow afternoon he will accompany her and her mother and aunt to their annual church picnic.

When Bev and Shirley have a morning off they like to take him out to lunch before he heads to the field. All agree he has a tremendous work ethic, showing up at the field early, going to the gym regularly, and keeping at it day after day, even though he has not played in many actual games this season. The team released him in late July, but he stayed on as the strength and conditioning coach. That he stuck with the team and hasn't tried to go somewhere else to play says a lot for his character, says Lori.

The other players who stayed with her had different options. Danny, whose last name she has forgotten, was with her only a week or two before being cut. Daryl Jones stayed about a month. Then he was traded to a team in Texas. A guy sitting a few seats over calls Lori the "kiss of death." She laughs. It isn't too far from the truth. Last season she went through fourteen players, and this season there have been quite a few as well. At present she has John and Curt. John was a trade for Matt Sanders. Matt was an infielder who was only with Lori, and the team, for about three days. He got traded for a pitcher, which the team desperately needed. He was eventually okay with the trade, but at first it was difficult. He hadn't been here long, and he didn't really want to pack up and go to a whole new team quite so soon. Of course, he didn't really have a choice.

Billy Mottram never had to worry about leaving the team.

His position was always secure, maybe a little too secure. The hope had been for him to break into affiliated ball. Now he just wants to finish the season as strong as he can. After it is all over he'll drive home to Massachusetts, take a month or so off, and then start training for next season. He isn't sure if he'll work as a substitute teacher again. His only real plans, besides training for next season, are to catch up with his English bulldog, Sophie, take a short trip to San Diego to see a friend, and wait to hear from manager Toby Rumfield about playing again next season.

He is less sure of himself than he was at the beginning of the season when he set the goal of hitting anywhere from fifteen to twenty home runs, batting in seventy to eighty runs, and stealing anywhere from thirty to forty bases. He'll end up finishing the season batting .260, with eight home runs, thirty-seven runs batted in, and twenty-two stolen bases. He doesn't have much of an explanation for why things turned out like they did except to say, "Baseball is a game of failure." He needs to get better at some things, work on his swing, but overall it wasn't anything in particular. "I just had one of those years," he says. "That's all."

It's the same kind of year the team had. Instead of competing for a playoff spot, Toby talks about winning forty games. Even that will be hard. Right now they have thirty-six wins with eight games left to play. To make forty they have to win half of their remaining games, a tough order for a team that has fifty-two losses. But it would make the season seem more respectable, says Toby, and closer to the forty-nine wins they had last season. "A little easier to swallow, I guess, if we could just see that forty mark," he says. It would also probably make his chances of coming back next season a little better. At this point, he says, the owner hasn't mentioned whether he wants him back. Toby is crossing his fingers.

It doesn't help. The Freedom ends up losing the game 8–3, and the following night, their last home game, they lose again, this time 6–3. Out of the eight remaining games Toby spoke of, they win only two, losing their last game, the one Tim's father drove out to see, 6–2. They finish the season with fifty-eight losses. They don't make the forty wins Toby had hoped for, instead pulling in only thirty-eight.

That is how their 2010 season ends. It will be both Tim Grogan's and Toby Rumfield's last. Tim not only gives up playing but also decides to turn down his front-office job and instead work in his mother's restaurant. Toby decides not to return after his wife, Kari, is offered a job as an assistant front-office general manager in affiliated baseball for the Class-A Short-Season Aberdeen IronBirds. When they married she had planned to follow Toby as he moved up the baseball ladder. Now it is he who is following her to Aberdeen, Maryland. That's when Toby gives up on his dream of coaching, at least for now.

22. Florence Freedom pitcher
Kevin Whittaker tosses a ball in the
clubhouse before a game. By James
Calvert.

23. (*Opposite top*) Florence Freedom
hometown player Tim Grogan gets
ready for a game. Hitting coach Pete
Rose Jr.'s jersey can be seen in the
background. By James Calvert.

24. (*Opposite bottom*) Florence Freedom hitting coach Pete Rose Jr. in
the batting cage with a player before
a game. By James Calvert.

25. (*Above*) Florence Freedom players wait outside their clubhouse to
be driven down the hill to the field
for a game. By James Calvert.

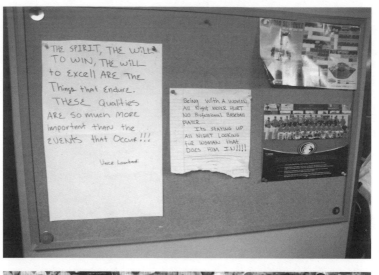

26. (*Top*) Florence Freedom clubhouse manager Randy Blaker likes to
post inspirational sayings and advice
in the clubhouse. By James Calvert.

27. Florence Freedom mascots Liberty the eagle and his sister, Belle,
enjoy a dance. By James Calvert.

28. The Wall Rats' official mascots.
By James Calvert.

29. Florence Freedom veteran player Tim Grogan's fiancée, Katie Sparrow (*far left*) sits in the stands with friends. By James Calvert.

Afterword

The 2010 professional baseball season in Kentucky can be summed up by the individual dreams it kindled and killed. Like anywhere in the Minor and independent league system, there were those players who excelled—and those who didn't. In Bowling Green Eligio "Eli" Sonoqui was on the cover of the Hot Rods' program one month and released the next. In Louisville Aroldis Chapman struggled at times but received a standing ovation before he even threw his first Major League pitch at the Great American Ballpark in Cincinnati on August 31. When the radar gun started hitting 100, the fans went crazy; it would top out at 103 that night. Aroldis tossed a perfect eighth inning in the Reds' 8–4 win over the Milwaukee Brewers for his Major League debut. After several wild appearances at the start of the 2011 season, Aroldis was placed on the disabled list for inflammation in his pitching shoulder. Matt Maloney started the 2011 season with the Reds as a relief pitcher before also spending time on the DL. Before the start of the 2012 season, Aroldis was transitioning toward becoming a starter next season, and Matt was picked up by the Minnesota Twins.

What differentiates those who made it from those who didn't? Talent, yes, but there are other factors as well. There are injuries and mind games and politics. Then there is life. And it keeps on going whether you're playing well or poorly, whether you're living your dream or watching it slip away.

In Kentucky Eli was not the only player to be disappointed during the 2010 season. Former big leaguer Chris Burke decided to call it quits for good after the Louisville Bats released him. Teammate Justin Lehr is hoping to come back, but had to sit out the season after undergoing Tommy John surgery.

In Florence Tim Grogan is hanging up his cleats, having never reached the Majors or even the higher levels of affiliated baseball. In Bowling Green Jairo De La Rosa had a lot of time to contemplate transitioning to a pitcher in a season he spent largely on the disabled list.

Then there are those players who moved a little closer to realizing their goals, like Bowling Green's Chris Murrill and Lexington's Jose Altuve, both of whom were promoted to Class-A (advanced) during the 2010 season. Jose was hitting so well at that level in 2011 that there was talk that he might be the Astros' best hitting prospect and made his Major League debut on July 20. Jiovanni Mier packed on twenty pounds, bringing his six-foot-two frame to two hundred pounds for the 2011 season, a gain that excited the Astros organization. Although he started the 2011 season back in Lexington, Jio's playing was much improved, and he finished the season in Class-A (advanced).

These changes may not play out before a large audience. But

that doesn't mean the hope and heartache aren't felt. Fans watch for the chance to see stars like Aroldis pitch 100-plus-mph fast balls. But they can relate to players like Justin who have seen success and failure and have the fortitude to keep believing day after day that it is all worthwhile. They watch him struggle to balance his personal dream of baseball with the reality of fatherhood and a family to support.

Will he play again? In late fall 2010 Justin was feeling "fantastic" and talking about being back in Louisville in April. He felt the surgery gave him a second chance to get back to the Majors. He started the 2011 season with the AA Carolina Lookouts and spent time on the DL for nerve irritation before moving up to the AAA Bats in late May. Before the end of the season, he was back in AA.

After a season shortened by injury, Jairo ended up needing shoulder surgery. His former Hot Rods teammate Eli Sonoqui enrolled in a yearlong course to be an auto technician after he was released in 2010. Fittingly, Eli chose to specialize in hot rods and classic muscle cars. He continued playing baseball in an adult men's league and planned to play in a winter league in Mexico, with hopes of eventually making it back to affiliated baseball in the United States. Businessman and longtime Hot Rods supporter Rick Kelley's dreams were derailed in a different way in 2011 when he suffered financial setbacks. Strength and conditioning coach Jared Elliott moved up, but broadcaster Tom Gauthier and trainer Scott Thurston were still with the Hot Rods in 2011. Tom was promoted to the AA New Hampshire Fisher Cats in the fall of 2011. His promotion did not come as a surprise, but the announcement that Lexington Legends president Alan Stein was retiring, also made in the fall of 2011, did. General manager Andy Shea was named Alan's replacement and finally opened his nighttime hot spot, TRUST Lounge, in September 2011.

Toby and Kari Rumfield moved from Florence, Kentucky, to Aberdeen, Maryland. Kari is as an assistant front-office general manager in affiliated baseball for the Class-A Short-Season Aberdeen IronBirds. In her official biography on the team's website she credits her love of baseball to her grandfather, who was a Minnesota Twins fan. She does not mention that her husband, Toby, used to play.

In February 2011 Billy Mottram and his pal Johnny Welch were traded to the Pittsfield Colonials of the Can-Am League in Massachusetts. It was the first time in years Billy would be playing so close to home, and he was excited that family and friends would finally be able to watch him.

Tim Grogan decided to give up his front-office job with the Freedom and instead work in his mother's restaurant. It is what he used to do in his off-season. Now he is no longer waiting for another season, another chance. But others are, and you can find them around the country, teaching in schools, bagging groceries, waiting tables, waiting until spring when the season starts and they have a chance to make it to the Majors.

Some of them will. The others will have this, a season in the lower levels playing as well as they can, doing a job they love and dreaming of something bigger.

Notes

INTRODUCTION

1. Mark Maloney, "Remembering Their First Steps," *Lexington Herald-Leader*, June 26, 1993.
2. Kentucky Educational Television, http://www.ket.org/kentuckylife/900s/kylife907.html, accessed September 2010.
3. Anne Jewell, *Baseball in Louisville* (Charleston SC: Arcadia, 2006).
4. Harry Rothgerber, Society for American Baseball Research, Kentucky Chapter, personal correspondence, 2010; and *Memories and Dreams* (National Baseball Hall of Fame) (Fall 2010).
5. http://web.minorleaguebaseball.com, accessed September 2010.

1. THE LEGEND BEHIND THE LEGENDS

1. http://donaldtermanpresents.com/baseballgrablexington.htm, accessed October 2010.
2. http://www.baseball-reference.com/bullpen/Kentucky-Illinois-Tennessee_League, accessed September 2010; http://www.base

ballreference.com/bullpen/Mountain_States_League, accessed
September 2010.

2. THE MAN WHO WOULD BE ALAN

1. Mark Maloney, "Legends Sale Completed for 'Clearly a Triple A
   Price,'" *Lexington Herald-Leader*, January 21, 2005.

5. GREAT EXPECTATIONS

1. Jewell, *Baseball in Louisville*.
2. Jewell, *Baseball in Louisville*.

7. THE FAITHFUL

1. http://www.baseballchapel.org, accessed September 2010.

9. THE STAR WHO ALMOST LANDED IN LOUISVILLE

1. Jewell, *Baseball in Louisville*.
2. Jewell, *Baseball in Louisville*.
3. Jewell, *Baseball in Louisville*.
4. Walter Barney, *Louisville's Baseball Milestones, 1865–1982* (pamphlet, 1982).

12. THE BUSINESSMEN

1. Rothgerber, personal correspondence, 2010; *Memories and Dreams*.
2. Frank Wakefield, Society for American Baseball Research, Kentucky Chapter, personal correspondence, 2010.

14. FALLING DOWN

1. Stories on Florence Freedom financing come from the *Cincinnati Enquirer*, *Lexington Herald-Leader*, and Associated Press, 2003–4.

16. STRIKE TWO

1. Kevin Eigelbach, "Florence Settles Lawsuit for $5M," *Cincinnati Post*, December 2, 2005.
2. Eigelbach, "Florence Settles Lawsuit for $5M."
3. Brenna Kelly, "League to Run Freedom," *Cincinnati Enquirer*, July 30, 2004.

4. Jennifer Edwards and Brenna Kelly, "Team Takes Another Strike," *Cincinnati Enquirer*, August 10, 2004; "City Sues to Evict Professional Baseball Team," Associated Press, August 24, 2004.
5. Cliff Peale, "Judge OKs New Freedom Capital Owner," *Cincinnati Enquirer*, December 15, 2004.